W9-CFM-190

2038

THE GREAT PYRAMID
TIMELINE PROPHECY

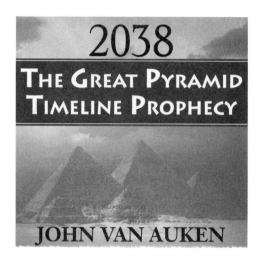

2038

THE GREAT PYRAMID TIMELINE PROPHECY

JOHN VAN AUKEN

4th Dimension Press ■ Virginia Beach ■ Virginia

CONTENTS

1

THE GREAT PYRAMID

The <u>Great Pyramid in</u> Egypt is the <u>only surviving member</u> of the <u>"Seven Wonders of the Ancient World."</u> The other six wonders were the Colossus of Rhodes, the Statue of Zeus at Olympia, the Mausoleum at Halicarnassus, the Hanging Gardens of Babylon, the Temple of Artemis (Diana) at Ephesus, and the Lighthouse at Alexandria.

Even in the modern world of today the Great Pyramid on the Giza Plateau is a marvel of design and engineering.

Sir Flinders Petrie (1853–1942), an English archaeologist known as the "father of modern Egyptology" wrote: "The pavement, lower casing and entrance passage are exquisitely wrought; in fact, the means employed for placing and cementing the blocks of soft limestone, weighing a dozen or twenty tons each, with such hair-like joints, are almost inconceivable at present; and the accuracy of the leveling is marvelous. How in the casing of the Great Pyramid, they could fill with cement a vertical joint about 5 feet by 7 feet in area, and only an average one-fiftieth

(1/50) part of an inch thick is a mystery. Yet this was the usual work over 13 acres of surface, with tens of thousands of casing stones, none less than a ton in weight." (30, p. 213)

W. Marsham Adams (1838–death date unknown), a British Egyptologist, fellow of Oxford's New College, wrote: "It is absolutely unique. No other building, it may be safely averred, contains any structure bearing the least resemblance to the upper chambers."(1, p. 34)

Architect James Fergusson (1808–1886), the 1871 recipient of the gold medal of the Royal Institute of British Architects, wrote in his book *The History of Architecture* (published in 1855) that the Great Pyramid is "the most perfect and gigantic specimen of masonry that the world has yet seen. No one can possibly examine the interior of the Great Pyramid without being struck with astonishment at the wonderful mechanical skill displayed in its construction. The immense blocks of granite brought from Syene [Aswan, in southern Egypt], a distance of 500 miles, polished like glass, are so fitted that the joints can scarcely be detected. Nothing can be more wonderful than the extraordinary amount of knowledge displayed in the construction of the discharging chambers over the roof of the principal apartment, in the alignment of the sloping galleries, in the provision of the ventilating shafts, and in all the wonderful contrivances of the structure. Nothing more perfect, mechanically, has ever been erected since that time." (18, p. 85)

Features of the Great Pyramid

There is no way to give all of the amazing features, mathematical wonders, and marvelous engineering feats of this pyramid without becoming overwhelmed. And there are plenty of books and Web sites that do this for you. But some of the more mysterious features should be noted here for they lend greater credence to the pyramid prophecy.

First among the mind–stretching facts about this wonder is the extraordinary degree of precision found throughout it. The architects and builders were more advanced than evolutionary theory would tolerate, given that everything old is primitive and we today are the apex of evolution. How could ancient primitives conceive of such a structure and then execute its building within tolerances that would be very difficult, if not impossible, to recreate today? We have already read the comments and the astonishment of some the experts who studied the edifice in the 1800s. Some of the most perplexing and mysterious features are:

- The Great Pyramid is positioned so exactly due north that it is more accurate than the modern attempt at the Paris Observatory, which is within 6 minutes of a degree of exact north. The ancient Great Pyramid is within 3 minutes of exact north and this after roughly four thousand years of settling (subsidence) and earthquakes! This is an astonishing achievement by ancient builders. It also appears to be positioned in alignment with specific stars above it! In an early announcement of this fact by Robert Bauval and Adrian Gilbert in their popular book *The Orion Mystery*, it was proposed to be in alignment with the star Alnitak in the Belt of Orion, and the other two Giza Plateau pyramids (Khafre and Menkaure) aligning with the other two stars in the Belt (Alnilam and Mintaka). Even the offset star Mintaka matched the offset Menkaure pyramid. (Note that two of the three pyramids are in-line with one another, but the third is slightly off-line. See illustration 1.) But after further investigation, it was found that this alignment was more of a mirror image, not a directly overhead match. Then another researcher, Andrew Collins in his book *The Cygnus Mystery*, revealed that many of the structures on the Giza Plateau, including the Great Pyramid, aligned precisely with Cygnus, the Swan Constellation. (See illustration 2.) How could these ancient people align their work with stars? And why would they attempt such a difficult feat?
- We have already read a bit about the precision with which the stones were cut and put together, but the cement used to hold these stones in place is unknown to scientifically oriented researchers. Even when our modern labs discovered the elements of the chemical composition of the cement, they were unable to duplicate it! How is this possible? From where did the ancient ones get this cement? How did they produce it, given their primitive conditions in comparison to ours? But wait, there's more! In 1986 a French research team found sand in a hidden chamber

behind the wall of the passageway to the Queen's Chamber, and when they examined the sand, it was found *not* to be indigenous to Giza! From where did the ancient ones get this sand? And why would they hide it in a secret chamber? Are they trying to convey some strange message to us? Aren't we the high point of evolution and science? These two discoveries add to the mystery and wonder of the Great Pyramid and the intentions of its ancient designers and builders.

- The red granite coffin (or sarcophagus) in the King's Chamber is too large to fit through the entrance to this chamber! Did these builders actually build this magnificent chamber *around* the coffin? If so, why? What purpose could justify adding so much difficulty to building the chamber? One might consider that they wanted to prevent the sarcophagus from ever being taken out of that chamber—but what a feat of engineering and manpower to build the massive chamber around the coffin. And what were they doing with this coffin that never contained a mummy and did not require a lid?

- There is growing evidence that the ancient Egyptians could not build this pyramid. It's true! Attempts have been made to prove that the pyramid could be constructed using known ancient Egyptian tools and methods. Egyptologist Dr. Mark Lehner made an attempt with a large group of people, but when the structure that he and his team built reached twenty feet high (six meters), they had to use a truck with a winch to get even the downsized stone blocks out of the quarry. They only attempted to cut and stack small blocks, so keep in mind that many of the stones in the Great Pyramid weigh from 2.5 to 70 tons and had to be hoisted to heights over four hundred feet! In the late seventies a Japanese team, funded by auto manufacturer Nissan, made another attempt to create a scaled-down model of the pyramid 59 feet high (18 meters) using the same primitive ancient Egyptian tools archaeologists assume were used, such as chisels and hammers. The highly skilled and technically savvy Japanese team could not cut the Aswan granite. They ended up using jackhammers. They were also unable to move the stones and ended up using bulldozers, a truck, and even a helicopter to get the blocks stacked in a pile that remotely resembled a pyramid. Again, like Dr. Lehner and his team, the Japanese used only small blocks, nothing close to the size and weight of those in the Great Pyramid. This situation is perplexing, without answers as to how this pyramid was built by these people. But even today we may not be able to build a structure like this because we have only two cranes on the planet that could possibly lift some of the stones in the pyramid to the heights necessary to place them on the levels they are found in that structure.

Clearly we are dealing with a people and a monument that is more than it appears to be. There are more details on this pyramid in the Appendices.

Historical Accounts of the Great Pyramid

Ca 1850 BC–1600 BC: One of the most important papyruses found in Egypt contains a plea, a lament, and a conversation between an Egyptian of the Old Kingdom called *Ipuwer* and God. The papyrus is called *The Dialogue of Ipuwer and the Lord of All* (formally titled *Papyrus Leiden I 344*, Leiden being the town in Netherlands where the papyrus is housed today). Here again we have a reproduction by a later generation of an earlier artifact for preservation and historical purposes—the papyrus was likely written in the New Kingdom, sometime in the 1200s BC, but Ipuwer lived sometime between 1850 BC and 1600 BC of the Middle Kingdom. Egyptologist Sir Alan Gardiner translated the papyrus into English in 1909 and considered it to be "a single picture of a particular moment in Egyptian history as it was seen by the pessimistic eyes of Ipuwer." (19, p. 8) What is of interest to us is Ipuwer's report that the Great Pyramid was forcibly broken into and its contents were removed while the upper chambers above the King's Chamber were also violently entered. Evidence of this is seen in the rough–cut passages that show no precision workmanship, not the earlier repair crew's well–cut passage into the original builders' stone. There are other rough–cut areas within the pyramid that indicate attempts to gain entry without concern for the structure, such as the damage to the large niche of the

Queen's Chamber by persons not concerned with precision. Archaeologist Sir Flinders Petrie wrote: "When, then, was the Pyramid first violated? Probably by the same hands that so ruthlessly destroyed the statues and temples of Khafra, and the Pyramids of Abu Roash, Abusir, and Sakkara. That is to say, probably during the civil wars of the seventh to the tenth dynasties." [ca 2181–2055 BC] (30, p. 217) Here's a passage from the Ipuwer Papyrus that appears to confirm the violence but not the date: "All is in ruin. A man kills his brother. Blood is everywhere. A few laws of the judgment hall are cast forth. Officials are slain and their records are taken away. The secrets of the kings of Upper and Lower Egypt are divulged. *What the pyramid concealed has become empty and the palace is destroyed*" (my italics). (19, p. 9)

24 BC: Greco-Roman geographer and historian Strabo recorded the only known firsthand witness to the original opening of the Great Pyramid. He wrote that there was an entrance on the South (he was confused because he was actually on the *North*) face that had a hidden door:

> "The Greater [pyramid], a little way up one side, has a stone that may be taken out, which being raised up (*sublato*, meaning to "take up" as in open upward), there is a sloping passage to the foundations." (38, pp. 84-5)

This is exactly how the original opening of the Great Pyramid is, and it is the entrance to the descending passageway that runs to the very foundation of the edifice.

Again we have an observation from Sir Flinders Petrie: "Strabo's account is less careful in the dimensions, merely giving roughly a stadium for the height and base of each of the larger Pyramids, and saying that one is a little larger than the other. As these dimensions vary from .85 to 1.25 stadia, he is, at least, quite as accurate as he professes to be. He gives the invaluable description of the Great Pyramid doorway, which so exactly accords with the only remaining doorway of a pyramid." (30, p. 160)

AD 250: Julius Solinus and others wrote about the phenomenon of the "consumption of the shadow," referring to a strange characteristic of the Great Pyramid's outer design that captures the sunlight such that it throws no shadow. When the original siding was on the structure, this occurred twice a day, in the morning at sunrise and the evening at sunset. It was because each side of the Great Pyramid slopes inward to an extremely precise center line, giving the edifice *eight* sides (see illustration 3) and the highly polished white limestone casing stones reflect the Sun's light. Many called these moments the "Flash" because it seemed as if the pyramid lit up brightly and no shadows were seen around it on the morning side at sunrise and then again on the evening side at sunset. What is most interesting about Solinus' writings is that he clearly confirms that in AD 250 the marvelous white limestone casing was still on the Great Pyramid. Today it is largely gone, removed by generations using it to build surrounding structures of the modern era. The exceptions that remain are of a few unpolished and dingy ones (see illustration 4).

AD 820: The entrance to the Great Pyramid that tourists use today was first cut by treasure-seeking Arabs led by Caliph al–Ma'mun, roughly around AD 820. A "caliph" (Arabic *khalifa*, meaning "successor") is a chief Islamic civil and religious ruler, regarded as the successor of Mohammed. The original entrance is just above al–Ma'mun's forced entrance.

Dating the Great Pyramid

The longstanding date for the construction of the Great Pyramid is 2560 BC during the reign of Pharaoh Khufu (Cheops in Greek), but there is some controversy in this dating.

There is an Egyptian stela (a rectangular, vertical slab of stone that commemorates events and persons) titled the "Inventory Stela" that was found in 1858 in the ruins of the temple of Isis at the southeastern foot of the Great Pyramid by Auguste Mariette, an Egyptologist and founder of the Egyptian Museum. The stela is dated to the Twenty–Sixth Dynasty (685–525 BC) but reports on Pharaoh Khufu's (Cheops in Greek) repairs to and construction of Giza plateau monuments that occurred between 2589 to 2566 BC in the Fourth Dynasty (subsequent generations often reproduced earlier artifacts for preservation and historical purposes, just as we do today). The reason this stela is important is because its inscription appears to indicate that the Great Pyramid and the Sphinx were already built when Khufu's activities were recorded on the stela. Keep in mind that no one could interpret Egyptian hieroglyphs until 1822 when Jean–François Champollion published the translation of the Rosetta Stone. Here's the translation of the Inventory Stela:

> The place of the Sphinx of Harmakhis [*Hr-m-y' kw t*, associated with the horizon and the sun; thus: *Sphinx of the Rising Sun*] is on the south of the house of Isis, Mistress of the Pyramid [it's already there]; on the north of Osiris, Lord of Rosta [*R3-st3* or *Rc-sTcw*, Rosta, or *Restau*, which means the "Mouth of the Passages," which is the entrance to the land of the dead]. He [Khufu] restored the statue [the Sphinx], all covered in painting of the guardian of the atmosphere, who guides the winds with his gaze. He replaced the back part of the Nemes headdress, which was missing, with gilded stone. The figure of this god, cut in stone, is solid and will last to eternity, keeping its face looking always to the East [in the direction of the rising Sun, the Sphinx's face looks East]. The writings of the goddess of Harmakhis [the rising Sun] were brought, in order to investigate. . . . may he grow; may he live forever and ever, looking toward the East.
>
> Live Horus Medjer [another name for Khufu), King of Upper and Lower Egypt; Khufu, who is given life. For his mother Isis, the Divine Mother, Mistress of The Western Mountain of Hathor [goddess of the principles of love, beauty, music, joy, and motherhood], he [Khufu] made [this] writing on a stela. He gave [Isis] a new sacred offering. He built [Isis] a House of stone [a stone temple], renewed the gods that were found in her temple. He found the house of Isis, Mistress of the Pyramid, beside the house of the Sphinx of [there's an unreadable word here] on the northwest of the house of Osiris, Lord of Rosta. He built his pyramid beside the temple of this goddess, and he built a pyramid for the king's-daughter Henutsen beside this temple. (4, p. 85)

This record of Khufu's activities can be interpreted to indicate that the Sphinx and the Great Pyramid were already built when he did some restoration, rebuilding, and new construction. Consider these lines: "He [Khufu] restored the statue [the Sphinx], all covered in painting of the guardian of the atmosphere, who guides the winds with his gaze. He replaced the back part of the Nemes headdress, which was missing, with gilded stone." And consider this passage: "He found the house of Isis, Mistress of the Pyramid, beside the house of the Sphinx . . . " Doesn't this indicate that the Great Pyramid was already standing? Then the stela states that Khufu built himself a pyramid and one for his daughter. Should we believe that the Great Pyramid is casually mentioned along with a daughter's pyramid, as if the two are in anyway equal? Nowhere on the stela is the grandeur and engineering of the Great Pyramid expressed.

Add to this that the only existing statue of Khufu, who is the supposed builder of the greatest monument in Egypt and one of the Seven Wonders of the Ancient World, is a three-inch tall, poorly carved piece of ivory. This little statuette was found headless in Abydos by Petrie in 1903. He whose men could carve granite could not carve a statue of their pharaoh in some significant size and in stone? This is not likely. If Khufu were the builder of this edifice, wouldn't there be statues and stelae everywhere proclaiming his greatness? But there is only this little ivory figurine.

Greek historian Herodotus (ca 484 BC–425 BC) wrote of Khufu (Cheops in Greek): "Cheops moreover came, they said, to such a pitch of wickedness, that being in want of money he caused his own daughter to sit in the stews [this means to prostitute herself], and ordered her to obtain from those who came a certain amount of money (how much it was, they did not tell me). And she not only obtained the sum appointed by her father, but also she formed a design for herself privately to leave behind her a memorial, and she requested each man who came in to give her one stone upon her building. And of these stones, they told me, the pyramid was built which stands in front of the great pyramid in the middle of the three, each side being one hundred and fifty feet in length." [Its sides are actually 160 feet in length.] (22, p. 124) From this account it appears that Herodotus was told that Khufu's daughter built the middle pyramid of the three so-called "Queens Pyramids" in front of the Great Pyramid for herself. However, archaeologists, particularly Drs. Lehner and Rainer Stadelmann consider it to belong to one of Khufu's wives, Queen Meritites (also spelled Mertiotes or Meretites). Archaeologists rarely consider personal historical reports about the sites from indigenous or closely associated persons of the time period, probably because they are so steeped in the evolutionary theory that all historical accounts are from less evolved persons.

Are we to believe that the greatest monument in Egypt and one of the greatest of the ancient world was built by a king who prostituted his daughter in order to pay for it?

Khufu may actually have overseen *repairs* to the Great Pyramid, for there is evidence of repair work in the King's Chamber and a relieving chamber above it. Whoever cut the passage that leads from the ceiling of the Grand Gallery to the lower relieving chamber, now called Davison's Chamber, left a neat, square-cut breakthrough passage in the stone of the original builders. The repair team also plastered over the cracks in the granite blocks above the King's Chamber. This work certainly appears to be that of a careful repair crew in antiquity, not treasure hunters.

Another key factor in dating the construction of the Great Pyramid is the intentional construction of the entrance and descending passageway to point like a telescope to the Earth's pole star. Astronomers have shown that the entrance and descending passageway pointed to Thuban (Alpha Draconis, α Draconis, α Dra) in its lower culmination in the years 3350 BC (long before Khufu) and again in 2170 BC (long after Khufu). Thuban was the pole star in antiquity (more on this later). The astronomer Richard A. Proctor (1837–1888) wrote: "Either of these [dates] would correspond with the position of the descending passage in the Great Pyramid; but Egyptologists tell us there can absolutely be no doubt that the later epoch [2170 BC] is far too late . . . " Proctor concludes: "If then we regard the slant passage as intended to bear on the Pole-star at its sub-polar passage, we get the date of the pyramid assigned as about 3350 years BC, with a probable limit of error of not more than 200 years either way, and perhaps of only fifty years." (41, p. 7) Clearly this date is long before Khufu; and what is even more important is that this date is before the so-called "Fourth Dynasty Pyramid Builders," dating from 2613–2498 BC, including "Khufu's" pyramid at the proposed date of 2550

BC. There's more evidence to support the idea that the Fourth Dynasty pharaohs were the *mastaba* builders (ancient Egyptian tomb in the form of a flat-roofed, rectangular structure) on the Giza Plateau rather than the pyramid builders.

Early in the career of the acclaimed Egyptologist Dr. Mark Lehner, who worked on the Giza Plateau most of his life, he carbon-dated the cement between the massive building blocks that compose the Great Pyramid. In order to get the most objective results, Dr. Lehner sent his samples to two different labs. To his amazement and that as well as the distress of many others, both labs dated the mortar from the bottom blocks of the pyramid to 1400 BC and the mortar from the top blocks of the pyramid to 3000 BC! Had the pyramid had been built upside down—its top before its bottom? Actually, the dates were more likely indications of when the mortar had been exposed to contaminating organic matter by the removal of the original covering stones. The Great Pyramid was surfaced with "casing stones" of highly polished white limestone. Very few of the original covering stones remain today. If these odd dates for the age of the mortar reveal the time when the covering stones were removed, then the top of the pyramid was exposed in 3000 BC—a date closer to the pole star alignment of 3350 BC and 450 years before Khufu existed.

Archaeologists point to an important piece of evidence supporting their view that Khufu built the Great Pyramid: his cartouche painted in red ochre in the relieving chambers above the King's Chamber. Archaeologists point to this as clearly indicating that the builders were working for Khufu. Here again we have a controversy; Walter M. Allen of Pittsburgh, Pennsylvania states that his great-grandfather was Humphries W. Brewer, who had been one of the stonemasons working with Howard Vyse, the discoverer of the red-paint Khufu cartouche. Allen states that he possessed family documents in which Brewer states that he witnessed a man named Hill, who was also working for Vyse, go into the pyramid with red paint and a brush. He said that Brewer objected to these forgeries but was then fired by Vyse and banned from the site. Brewer later worked for the German Egyptologist Lepsius and tried to examine the marks inside the pyramid but was refused permission by Vyse. Adding to this story is that Howard Vyse drew the cartouche of Khufu in his own journal in 1837 incorrectly spelled! However, the argument that the red ink cartouche is or was once misspelled is also controversial because there were other journals at the time of Howard Vyse that show it spelled correctly. Furthermore, a portion of one of the red ink marks is supposedly behind an original stone, making it unlikely that anyone in the 1800s could have drawn it, unless he intentionally made it *appear* as if it were behind the original stone.

Let's move on to the discovery of the timeline inside this pyramid and its eventual correlation to the *Egyptian Book of the Dead.*

2

DISCOVERING THE TIMELINE

For many years much attention has been and continues to be given to the Mayan prophecy of 2012—how the Mayan Long Count Calendar ended a 13-Baktun cycle on the Winter Solstice, December 21-23, 2012 and how Mayan astronomical observations identified a rare alignment of our sun in the exact center of the Milky Way Galaxy when viewed from Earth in our present time—a celestial event that occurs only every 25,826.54 years. But little attention has been given to the ancient Egyptian prophecy found in the Great Pyramid in Giza, Egypt. Like the Mayan prophecy, the Great Pyramid prophecy also points to these present times. Surprisingly, in the 1800s and early 1900s much of this timeline inside the Great Pyramid was well known and much was written about it. Some of the most important scientists and researchers of that time had detailed knowledge of this timeline and how it correlated with content in the *Egyptian Book of the Dead*. Eventually, points along the timeline were associated with world events, taking it to the level of a prophecy about humankind's journey through material incarnations.

How was this timeline and its prophecy discovered? There were two ways. The first factor dealt with the design of the interior of the Great Pyramid which was unlike anything ever found around the globe in antiquity and would be nearly impossible to recreate today. Therefore, the minds that studied the pyramid's unusual features and amazing craftsmanship knew it had to be more than simply a tomb.

Researcher W. Marsham Adams wrote: "That its various features are meaningless, or the mere result of caprice, is a suggestion to which the forethought and lavishness of the calculation displayed in every detail unmistakably gives the lie. Nor again can we maintain that they are necessary for the purposes of an ordinary tomb. For, they are not to be found in other pyramids which were used for that purpose." (1, p. 34)

Adams' last statement that they were not ordinary tombs is correct, because none of the major pyramids in Egypt contained a mummy—none. The Great Pyramid and perhaps all of the major Egyptian pyramids, as well as their intricate passageways and chambers were more likely used for active services and ceremonies. Given their apparent association with death, the pyramids may well have been used for death-like initiations or for preparing select individuals for dying and death and subsequent activity after death.

W. Marsham Adams knew this because in his publication, *The Book of the Master*, quoting from a letter by Sir Gaston Maspero, Adams identifies "the prevalence of a tradition among the priests of Memphis" that "the Secret House [Great Pyramid] was the scene where the neophyte was initiated into the mysteries." (1, p. 179)

Archaeologists concede that no mummy was ever found in any of the major pyramids in Egypt and the sarcophagus in the Great Pyramid never had a lid.

The second factor that contributed to finding the timeline inside the Great Pyramid was the discovery of a measurement associated with the construction of this pyramid. In 1646, John Greaves, professor of astronomy at Oxford, published his *Pyramidographia* in which he first theorized that the Great Pyramid at Giza was constructed by a geometric cubit, which he called the "Memphis cubit." In 1737, the antiquarian Thomas Birch published research papers based on Greaves' hypothetical cubit. Even Sir Isaac Newton (1642–1727) used Greaves' measurements of the Great Pyramid and published them in a paper entitled "A Dissertation upon the Sacred Cubit." In this paper Newton correlated the "Memphis cubit" to the cubit in the Bible. This measurement and its association with the Bible fired up religiously oriented researchers, particularly Christian researchers, who found many correlates between Egyptian theology and Judeo–Christian concepts and stories (i.e., such as an immaculate conception of the Messiah, Isis conceiving Horus without copulation, and then Horus overcoming Satan, who was *Set* in Egyptian lore). These researchers began investigating with a more religious view. They were also aided by the translation of the Rosetta Stone (1822), making the *Egyptian Book of the Dead* of readable. It wasn't long before the measurement and the esoteric elements of the *Egyptian Book of the Dead* were united. Sir Gaston Maspero (1846–1919), the famous French Egyptologist, professor of archaeology, and developer of the Egyptian Museum in Cairo, explained, "The [Great] pyramid and *The Egyptian Book of the Dead* reproduce the same original, the one in words, the other in stone." (12, p. 88)

This theory, along with other ideas, became known as *Pyramidology*. Two essential elements of pyramidology were: (1) that the ancient Egyptian theology and cosmology, both highly moral and spiritual, asserted that human beings were "godlings" formed by the Creator of the entire universe and were destined to return to that condition; and (2) that the amazing construction of the Great Pyramid was done intentionally to preserve a hidden prophecy about these godlings, their journey through evolution, and their ultimate destiny among the stars of the heavens. Judeo–Christian theology—of which most of these early researchers were adherents—considered humans to have been originally created in the image of God (Genesis 1:26–27), and Christians believed that Jesus Christ affirmed human godliness in his statement in the Gospel of John 10:34: "Is it not written in your law, 'I said, you are gods?'" The law he is referring to is found in Psalm 82:6: "You are gods, sons of the Most High, all of you . . . ." Additionally, Egypt had a major role in the Bible stories that most of these researchers accepted as truth. There was even a verse in the Bible that pyramidologists believed was referring to the Great Pyramid of Giza, Egypt. (More on this later.)

The Judeo–Christian influence came early on via the Coptic Christians, who were the descendants of the ancient Egyptians. Islam did not arrive in Egypt until six hundred years after Christ. Researcher and author David Davidson believed that from the *Egyptian Book of the Dead* the Coptic Christians drew the mystical and allegorical elements that were introduced into early Christian Gnosticism. Christian Gnosticism contains pyramidal figures and astronomical concepts. David Davidson attributes the survival of the ancient Egyptian calendar, the names of the months, the dialect, and the assistance in elucidating the translation of ancient hieroglyphic texts to the Coptic knowledge of ancient Egypt. Davidson quotes Dr. Alois (Aloys) Sprenger (1813–1896, a prominent scholar of Oriental studies), who is quoted in Howard Vyse's Appendix to *Operations Carried on at the Pyramids of Gizeh in 1837, Volume II*, "the traditions of the ancient Egyptians were preserved by their descendants, the Copts, who were held in great esteem by the Arabs [initially, not so much lately] . . . It may be remarked that the Arabian authors have given the same accounts of the Pyramids [sic], with little or no variation, for above a thousand years; and that they appear to have repeated the traditions of the ancient Egyptians, mixed up with fabulous stories and incidents, certainly not of Mahometan [Mohammedan] invention." (40, p. 387) One of these Arabian accounts is by Masoudi, whose manuscript is in the archives of Oxford University, and goes like this: "He [Pharaoh Surid, believed by the Coptics and Arabs to have built the two major pyramids on the Giza Plateau] also order the priests to deposit within them [the pyramids] written accounts of their [Egyptian] wisdom and acquirements in the different arts and sciences . . . with the writings of the priests containing all manner of wisdom, the names and properties of medical plants, and the sciences of arithmetic and geometry, that they might remain as records for the benefit of those who could afterwards comprehend them . . . In the Eastern Pyramid [which is the Great Pyramid] were inscribed the heavenly spheres and figures representing the stars and planets . . . The king also deposited . . . the positions of the stars and their cycles; together with the history and chronicle of time past, of that which is to come, and every future event which would take place in Egypt." (40, p. 321)

Egyptian historian al-Maqrizi, also known as Makrizi (1364–1442), wrote from Coptic sources that "the first pyramid [the Great] was especially dedicated to history and astronomy; the second [pyramid] to medical knowledge." (40, p. 354)

Researchers and authors David Davidson and H. Aldersmith published in 1924 a large book titled *The Great Pyramid: Its Divine Message*. In this book the prophecy timeline was meticulously detailed and correlated to known world events and supposed future events. Davidson first got the idea of a timeline from W. Marsham Adams, author of *The House of the Hidden Places: A Clue to the Creed of the Egyptians* (1895) and *The Book of the Master* (1898). Adams wrote that "the unique system of passages and chambers in the Great Pyramid have little meaning as a tomb but have an allegorical significance only explained by referring to the *Egyptian Book of the Dead*." (12, p. iii) When we think about this, if the Great Pyramid were only a tomb for the pharaoh, it would not need so many passageways, chambers, and unusual features; such as the Great Step, the granite "veil" stone in the antechamber to the King's Chamber, and the distinctive elements of the pyramid's subterranean portion. Adams wrote that select chapters in the *Egyptian Book of the Dead* refer to an "ideal structure and to the passages and chambers therein, and that these passages and chambers followed precisely the order and description of those of the Great Pyramid." (12, p. 88)

The exact translation of the original title of the *Egyptian Book of the Dead* is *The Book of Coming Forth into the Light* (often translated *Coming Forth by Day*). And since the Great Pyramid was called *Ta Khut*, meaning "The Light," you can see how some portions of the papyrus texts might relate to the Great Pyramid, especially since the *Egyptian Book of the Dead* describes passages, halls, chambers, transitions, tests, dangerous or even wrong turns, and various gates through which the dead must make their way—or through which initiates receive training about life beyond death.

Likely influenced by the popular *Tibetan Book of the Dead*, the German Egyptologist Karl Richards Lepsius, the first translator of the papyrus texts, labeled the whole collection *Egyptian Book of the Dead*. Curiously, the *Tibetan Book of the Dead* is actually titled *Bardo Thodol*, which in Tibetan means *liminality liberation*, akin to "threshold of liberation." Its title is often transliterated as *Liberation through Hearing during the Intermediate State*.

Both of these books are about consciousness and activity in the Netherworld or the realm of the dead. However, both appear to also have much information for the incarnate to use in becoming aware of the nonphysical realms of life beyond this physical reality and may therefore also be useful for experiencing the realms beyond the physical while in physicality. The fact that ancient people were so interested in the life after death of the physical body has added to this theory that the Great Pyramid with its many passageways, chambers, and unusual features may have been used to initiate incarnate souls into the other dimensions of life.

W. Marsham Adams likely got some of his ideas from Professor Charles Piazzi Smyth, Astronomer Royal of Scotland from 1846 to 1888. (Piazzi Smyth was the pioneer of the modern practice of placing telescopes at high altitudes to enjoy the best observing conditions.) Professor Smyth and his wife Jessie (who accompanied him on all of his travels) camped next to the Great Pyramid to measure the exterior and interior of the amazing edifice. Professor Smyth published his book *Our Inheritance in the Great Pyramid in 1864* and expanded it over the years. This

book is also titled in some editions, *The Great Pyramid: Its Secrets and Mysteries Revealed.* Smyth claimed that the measurements he obtained from the Great Pyramid revealed the "pyramid inch," equivalent to 1.001 British inch. He believed it was the standard of measurement used by the architects of the ancient structure. Smyth also believed that the pyramid inch was a divinely inspired measurement handed down from the time of Shem, one of Noah's three sons who are Shem, Ham, and Japheth and whose descendants eventually became seventy nations (Genesis 10). Shem's descendants became the Semitic populations which include most all Middle Eastern peoples; this would also contain the Jews and Arabs, as well as many others in antiquity. While measuring the pyramid, Smyth wrote that he found the number of inches in the perimeter of the base equal to one thousand times the number of days in a year, and he found a numeric relationship between the height of the pyramid in inches to the distance between Earth and the Sun in miles. (He also wrote that "proceeding around the globe due north and due south of the Great Pyramid . . . there is more earth and less sea in that meridian than in any other meridian all the equator round." He also wrote that "taking the distribution of land and sea in parallels of latitude, there is more land-surface in the Great Pyramid's general parallel of 30° than in any other."(33, p. 89) And he made attractive and often reprinted maps to support his statements. Unfortunately, when carefully measured, neither of these statements appears to be correct. And there were other pronouncements from various pyramidologists that proved to be incorrect, such as the authoritative statement that the sarcophagus in the King's Chamber and the Ark of the Covenant in the Bible have the same volume—adding a biblical and godly connection between the pyramid and the Bible. Here are the dimensions and volumes of the two famous artifacts. As we can see, the Ark has much less volume than the sarcophagus.

Sarcophagus (interior)	Ark of the Covenant (exterior)
Length = 6.51 feet	Length = 3.75 feet
Width = 2.23 feet	Width = 2.25 feet
Depth = 2.87 feet	Height = 2.25 feet
Volume = 41.67 cubic feet	Volume = 18.98 cubic feet

Thus, the theory that the Great Pyramid contained a prophecy that could be revealed by detailed measurements and correlated with verses in the *Egyptian Book of the Dead* was thrown into doubt as a result of these inaccurate statements by many of the original pyramidologists. Unfortunately, many, many people have repeated these mistaken claims for years, even today.

Nevertheless, before throwing the whole of pyramidology out the window, let's continue with our exploration into the timeline prophecy.

In 1910 while calculating and measuring the prophecy inside the Great Pyramid, David Davidson and H. Aldersmith used a measurement now known as the "pyramid inch," which was derived from John Greaves' original work with the sacred cubit. Subsequent pyramidologists and even anti-pyramidologists, such as Petrie, affirmed that the 25-inch sacred cubit was clearly used in the construction of the Great Pyramid.

For David Davidson this use of the sacred cubit in the construction of the edifice was clear evidence that the measuring units did not originate in Egypt and that another more ancient culture using an oral tradition and meeting a cataclysmic end brought the wisdom to Egypt. Here's Davidson: "The fact that these systems were derived from the scale of the Sacred Cubit of 25 P. inches again confirms that the Egyptian units of measure were not formulated in Egypt. The sacred system and its derived Egyptian Units all clearly belong to the period of the former civilization . . . " (12, p. 70) To support his position Davidson points out that the major ancient cultures all have a legend of a prior culture which met its end in a manner that was devastating. He writes: "In ancient Egypt, the tradition exists as 'The Destruction of Mankind,' in ancient Mexico and Peru as 'The Destruction of the World,' and in Babylonia and Assyria, and in China, as 'The Deluge.' These traditional accounts, when compared, indicate they are various versions of the Noachian [Noah] Deluge narrative in the Hebrew Book of Genesis." (12, p. 39) Davidson clarifies his comments in a footnote stating, "It must always be remembered, however, that in all stages and periods of civilization the highest forms exist alongside the primitive and barbarous. Even the best authorities permit themselves to forget this." (12, p. 39)

The length of a pyramid inch is not only a portion of the sacred cubit but is also the space on the underside of a stone relief in the antechamber to the King's Chamber, known as the "boss mark" (see illustration 5). The boss mark is in the shape of a solar disk setting on the horizon; therefore the bottom portion of its circle is under the horizon, and the flat bottom of this solar disk is a depth of one "pyramid inch"—the flat space between the base of the slab upon which the boss mark appears and the outer surface of this projected solar disk.

There are critics of this measurement, such as the famous Sir William Flinders Petrie (best known as Flinders Petrie), who wrote in 1883, "This boss on the leaf is very ill-defined, being anything between 4.7 and 5.2 [inches] wide, and between 3.3 and 3.5 high on its outer face." Petrie felt that "this boss, of which so much has been made by theorists, is merely a rough projection, like innumerable others that may be seen; left originally for the purpose of lifting the blocks." (30, p. 78) Despite Petrie's opinion, the slab and the boss relief are more than a lifting mechanism.

The slab is in one of three specialized grooves in the antechamber to the King's Chamber and appears to be the only surviving remnant of what were once three slabs. And the rising solar disk is not likely a lifting device since, as reported by John and Morton Edgar in their expedition from 1904–1909 in *Great Pyramid Passages: Part II, Letters from Egypt and Palestine,* "The granite leaf appears to be an inch narrower than its corresponding grooves in the wainscots . . . Close examination shows that this difference is made up by narrow one-inch projections or rebates on the north face of the leaf, which make it fit tightly into its grooves. With the exception of these rebates (which are evidence of special design), the whole of the north face of the leaf has been dressed or planed down one inch, in order that one little part in the middle might appear in relief." (13, p. 302) It is an intentional relief, a glyph containing a precise measurement for discovering the architects' fundamental measuring unit, as well as the prophecy hidden in the pyramid.

One should also keep in mind that Flinders Petrie's father William (1821–1908, the son of Captain Matthews Flinders, the explorer and cartographer of Australia—its runs in the family) was a pyramidologist! This possibly motivated Flinders to show his father how science and evolution were the better truth and that pyramidology, with its religious and messianic undertones, was a delusion of the religiously inclined. Curiously, many of Flinders' exactingly accurate measurements served to support the themes of pyramidology (using steel tapes and special chains 1200 inches long, Flinders Petrie measured the pyramid with amazing accuracy).

David Davidson believed the pyramid inch measurement (which he also called the "primitive inch") was supported by many more features in, on, and above the Great Pyramid than the boss mark, stating that the obvious connection between a unit of measurement and a chronograph is the astronomical cycles associated with the Great Pyramid's exterior. He writes, "There is the cycle of the Precessions of the Equinoxes, associated in the pyramid's geometry with a standard period of reference of 25,826.54 Solar years. And there is the cycle of the revolution of the Autumnal Equinox from perihelion to perihelion. There is also the cycle defining the variations in the eccentricity of the Earth's orbit." (12, p. 140) He goes on with many more examples of how the pyramid is associated with time and the passage of time.

⟨From passages in the *Egyptian Book of the Dead*, pyramidologists concluded that the pyramid inch not only correlates to a measure of space in the stone structure but also to a measure of *prophetic time*. The measurement equals one year in time, from the original entrance to the Great Pyramid, through the descending and ascending passageways until reaching the "Great Step" at the top of the Grand Gallery. From that point on, the inch equals one month in time rather than one year. Time speeds up—the same amount of activities happen in one-twelfth of the time they used to take. ⟩

According to this model and its biblical connections, the pyramid timeline covers a period beginning with the descent of human souls as "the morning stars" spoken of in the biblical book of Job 38:7 ("When the morning stars sang together, and all the sons of God shouted for joy?") to a resurrection period when all the souls ascend to the heavens from whence they came ("And no one has ascended into heaven, but he that descended out of heaven, even the Son of man, who is in heaven." John 3:13) passing through metaphysical gates, passageways, and chambers of tests and developmental activities. Like this biblical passage of "morning stars," the ancient Egyptians believe that each human had a Star-body and a Star-being deep within him. (More on this in chapter 4.)

The last date in the pyramid timeline is 2038, indicating the end of the prophecy as it is recorded in the Great Pyramid.

But all of this information—the correlation between the *Egyptian Book of Dead* and features inside the Great Pyramid, the boss mark measuring device, and the prophetic timeline—became entangled with the collection of religious and biblical associations under the banner of *Pyramidology*. Eventually, degreed archaeologists as well as serious researchers divided themselves into two main groups: (1) the scientific group that saw nothing more than ancient remnants of a culture obsessed with surviving death, and in the context of the theory of evolution, these ancient ones had primitive superstitions and mythological tales; and (2) a mystical group of modern researchers who believed that God had a hand in building the Great Pyramid, that the Bible spoke of the Great Pyramid, that the *Egyptian Book of the Dead* was an allegorical record related to places inside the Great Pyramid, and that the timeline draws a parallel to events in world history now and in the future.

They quickly broke into two hard-and-fast positions wherein the scientific group gained the upper hand and the accepted view of ancient Egypt.

Before we leave this, let's review a little more about the development of pyramidology.

We know that Professor Smyth's correspondence with John Taylor (1781–1864) influenced his research significantly. John Taylor was a partner in a London publishing firm, and in 1859 he published his own book, *The Great Pyramid: Why Was It Built? And Who Built It?* Taylor never visited the pyramid, but the more he studied its structure, the more he became convinced that its architect was an Israelite acting under God's guidance, not an Egyptian. John Taylor was an influential man, and two biographies were written about him. He was also the publisher of the works of the famous English romantic poet John Keats.

Taylor claimed that the measurements in and around the Great Pyramid indicated that the ancients had used a unit of measure about 1/1000 greater than a modern British inch. This was the origin of the "pyramid inch." Taylor regarded the pyramid inch to be 1/25 of the sacred cubit whose existence had earlier been postulated by Sir Isaac Newton. The principal argument was that the total length of the four sides of the pyramid would be 36,524 (100 times the number of days in a year) if measured in pyramid inches.

The same year that Taylor's book was published (1859), Darwin's book *On the Origin of the Species* was published. And it was truly a time of point-counterpoint on the issue of evolution and its "up-from-the-apes" views versus the spiritual nobility of humanity and divine creation.

Taylor proposed that the Hyksos, literally *foreign rulers*, had built the Great Pyramid under the leadership of the High Priest Melchizedek. Hyksos was a term which he and others often incorrectly translated as "shepherd kings" and had incorrectly assumed that they were the Israelites (Genesis 14:18). But there is much evidence indicating that the Hyksos were Syrian–Palestinian migrants and soldiers who only seized the northeastern portion of the Nile River Delta, never governing enough of Egypt to build the pyramids on the west bank of the Nile at Giza.

Additionally, Professor Smyth and others believed that the people of Great Britain are the descendants of the Ten Lost Tribes of Israel. Of the original Twelve Tribes, ten "disappeared" from historical accounts after the invasion of Israel by the Assyrians in 732 BC and again in 720 BC, completely destroying the northern kingdom of Israel. This did not affect the southern kingdom of Judah and Jerusalem and the Temple. That destruction came later when Babylon invaded in 586 BC. Interestingly, in the south, the city of Jerusalem actually grew during the Assyrian invasions and occupations of the north, and many members of the northern tribes migrated to Jerusalem to avoid Assyrian capture and deportation. Given the information available, it is difficult to identify exactly which of the twelve tribes were "lost," but the seven northern tribes (Reuben, Issachar, Zebulun, Dan, Naphtali, Gad, and Asher) are all considered to be among the "lost" tribes. Since the tribe of Joseph, which had divided into the two sub-tribes of Ephraim and Manasseh, lived directly in the path of the Assyrian invading forces, much of it was "lost"; actually they came under Assyrian rule. That would leave the four tribes of Judah, Simeon, Benjamin, and Levi; and it is known that all these southern tribes were not affected by the invasion. However, the tribe of Simeon "disappeared" by being *integrated* into the tribe of Judah, so one could think of it as being among the lost tribes. Actually only nine tribes were "lost": Reuben, Issachar, Zebulun, Dan, Naphtali, Gad, Asher, Ephraim, and Manasseh. However, Assyrian and biblical records indicate that in the 732 BC invasion Reuben, Gad, and western Manasseh were captured and resettled in Assyria, not Britain. A portion of Ephraim, including the city of Janoah, was captured and ruled by an Assyrian governor; few were resettled. In the 720 BC reinvasion, massive deportation of the people of Israel did occur and was documented. It was because these tribes kept appointing their own kings despite Assyrian authority! But, here again, records indicate that many were sent to Assyria (the lands of modern-day Iraq). Even so, there is also evidence that the seafaring Phoenicians, Cypriots, and even Philistines helped many Israelites of the northern tribes escape by sea, sending them to lands in Western Europe, Britain, and Scandinavia. This gave the pyramidologists in Egypt (particularly the British ones) a sense of their personal, historical involvement in biblical Egypt.

The Scripture that was pointed to most often by pyramidologists was Isaiah 19: 19-20: "In that day there will be an altar to the Lord in the midst of the land of Egypt, and a pillar to the Lord at its border. It will be a sign and a witness to the Lord of hosts in the land of Egypt . . . " Pyramidologists believe that this passage is speaking of the Great Pyramid when it refers to "an altar to the Lord" and "a pillar to the Lord," but a pyramid is hardly an "altar" or "pillar" and it is not on the border. In his book *A Study in Pyramidology*, Raymond Capt states that the Hebrew word translated as "pillar," *matstsebah*, is "correctly translated *monument*." However, I could find no Hebrew Lexicon that translated matstsebah as anything other than a pillar or tree stump. However, matstsebah can be a pillar that is a "monument" to someone or some event, but it is in no way a massive pyramidal structure. Now some correlate this Hebrew word with the Arab word *mastaba*, which is a low, rectangular structure with an underground tomb. But the primitive root word from which matstsebah comes is *natsab*, which is associated with "standing," like a stanchion or pillar, or to "take a stand" or "take an upright position." This is an example of how pyramidologists too often stretched some facts to better fit their theories and to connect their theories with sacred Scripture—when it was unnecessary because what they had was sufficiently profound and meaningful.

When we read this often quoted passage from Isaiah *in context* with the whole of the chapter, it does not appear to be speaking about the Great Pyramid but rather an offering altar to Yahweh and the pillar of a spiritual person or persons who will lead the people closer to God. Here is chapter 19 of Isaiah (Revised Standard Version, RSV):

> An oracle concerning Egypt: Behold, the Lord is riding on a swift cloud and comes to Egypt; and the idols of Egypt will tremble at his presence, and the heart of the Egyptians will melt within them. And I will stir up Egyptians against Egyptians, and they will fight, every man against his brother and every man against his neighbor, city against city, kingdom against kingdom; and the spirit of the Egyptians within them will be emptied out, and I will confound their plans; and they will consult the idols and the sorcerers, and the mediums and the wizards; and I will give over the

Egyptians into the hand of a hard master; and a fierce king will rule over them, says the Lord, the Lord of hosts. And the waters of the Nile will be dried up, and the river will be parched and dry; and its canals will become foul, and the branches of Egypt's Nile will diminish and dry up, reeds and rushes will rot away. There will be bare places by the Nile, on the brink of the Nile, and all that is sown by the Nile will dry up, be driven away, and be no more. The fishermen will mourn and lament, all who cast hook in the Nile; and they will languish who spread nets upon the water. The workers in combed flax will be in despair, and the weavers of white cotton. Those who are the pillars of the land will be crushed, and all who work for hire will be grieved. The princes of Zo'an [area in the Nile Delta] are utterly foolish; the wise counselors of Pharaoh give stupid counsel. How can you say to Pharaoh, 'I am a son of the wise, a son of ancient kings'? Where then are your wise men? Let them tell you and make known what the Lord of hosts has purposed against Egypt. The princes of Zo'an have become fools, and the princes of Memphis [area just before the Delta, near Saqqara] are deluded; those who are the cornerstones of her tribes have led Egypt astray. The Lord has mingled within her a spirit of confusion; and they have made Egypt stagger in all her doings as a drunken man staggers in his vomit. And there will be nothing for Egypt which head or tail, palm branch or reed, may do. In that day the Egyptians will be like women, and tremble with fear before the hand which the Lord of hosts shakes over them. And the land of Judah will become a terror to the Egyptians [this would indicate a time long after the Great Pyramid was constructed]; everyone to whom it is mentioned will fear because of the purpose which the Lord of hosts has purposed against them. In that day there will be five cities in the land of Egypt that speak the language of Canaan and swear allegiance to the Lord of hosts [Genesis 14:2 tells us their names: Sodom, Gomorrah, Admah, Zeboiim, and Zoar (or Bela)]. One of these will be called the City of the Destruction. [One of the Dead Sea Scrolls changes "City of Destruction" to "City of Sun," and most modern Bibles use this more positive term. In Hebrew, *heres* is "sun" and *hheres* is "destruction." Since Zoar is the only city that is spared in the Bible story (Genesis 15:16), it is believed to be the City of Sun. But the City of the Sun may also be the Egyptian Heliopolis; literally, "city of the sun."] In that day there will be an altar to the Lord in the midst of the land of Egypt, and a pillar to the Lord at its border [to the Promised Land]. It will be a sign and a witness to the Lord of hosts in the land of Egypt; when they cry to the Lord because of oppressors he will send them a savior, and will defend and deliver them. And the Lord will make himself known to the Egyptians; and the Egyptians will know the Lord in that day and worship with sacrifice and burnt offering [the altar?], and they will make vows to the Lord and perform them. And the Lord will smite Egypt, smiting and healing, and they will return to the Lord, and he will heed their supplications and heal them. In that day there will be a highway from Egypt to Assyria, and the Assyrian will come into Egypt, and the Egyptian into Assyria, and the Egyptians will worship with the Assyrians. In that day Israel will be the third with Egypt and Assyria, a blessing in the midst of the earth, whom the Lord of hosts has blessed, saying, "Blessed be Egypt my people, and Assyria the work of my hands, and Israel my heritage." (Isaiah 19)

It is difficult to see how the Great Pyramid is spoken of in this chapter.

Extremists on either side of this debate took their points to such a degree that there was no room for reasonable elements of the other side's theories. In the case of the pyramidology, the biblical side of this debate often espoused positions that were simply not supportable by any existing evidence. In this case, even good evidence of a prophetic timeline inside the Great Pyramid and a correlation with chapters in the *Egyptian Book of the Dead* were dismissed along with the rest of the pyramidological theories. Gradually, even reasonable researchers had to leave any part of pyramidology alone, casting it into pseudoscience, or worse, sheer fiction. It became taboo. Today, no archaeologists in their right minds would present a paper on the correlation of the Great Pyramid with the *Egyptian Book of the Dead*—not if they wanted to keep their position at a university or on an authorized expedition team approved by Islamic Egyptian authorities.

Yet, our story requires that we sift through the muck and mire of pyramidology for the gold nuggets, and so we continue.

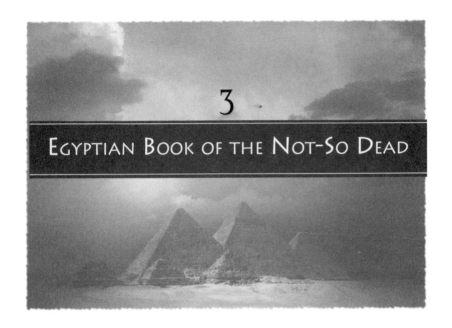

3

EGYPTIAN BOOK OF THE NOT-SO DEAD

The *content* in the *Egyptian Book of the Dead* dates to *before* the pharaohs, the pyramids, and the papyruses (papyri). In remote antiquity the content existed orally. They were called "utterances," only to be spoken as part of a spell-like invocation. They contained "words of power" (*hekau*). On a coffin lid containing a copy of this ancient content there is written *djed-medu*, which may be interpreted as "words to be spoken." Even the earliest *inscribed* texts of the *Egyptian Book of the Dead* contain portions indicating that they had been composed and revised long before the earliest known pharaohs.

The utterances were first carved on pyramid walls in Saqqara. Scholars agree that the "Pyramid Texts," as they are called, belong to a much earlier people and that priests of the subsequent dynastic periods had received them orally as part of sacred lore. Only later had the words become inscribed on the walls of select pyramids. Of such antiquity were these utterances that the scribes carving the hieroglyphics were perplexed over the origin of the texts and their meaning. [Reported by Gaston Maspero, "La Religion Égyptienne," 1884, in *Revue de l'Histoire des Religions*, t. xii. p. 125.] Yet, the scribes knew these texts were of vital importance and the priests overseeing the inscriptions expressed reverence concerning the texts. (See illustration 6.)

The pyramid texts were first discovered by French Egyptologist Sir Gaston Maspero in 1881. They are found in the pyramid of Unas (Fifth Dynasty; Unas likely ruled from 2375 to 2345 BC, but some date this pyramid to 3333 BC; Unas can also be written Unis). They are also found in the pyramid of Teti (Sixth Dynasty; Teti likely ruled from 2357? to 2332? BC and can also be written as Teta). They are found in the pyramids of Pepi I (2332 to 2283 BC) and Pepi II (2278 BC to 2184 BC) and in the pyramid of Merenra (2260 to 2254 BC). Each of these pyramids is located near the Step Pyramid of Djoser (pronounced *zo-ser*, dating to the Third Dynasty 2630 BC).

Who were the predynastic people that maintained the oral tradition? They may be those people who built and used the so-called "Egyptian Stonehenge," an assembly of huge stone slabs in the southern Sahara Desert in an area known as *Nabta* and dates to about 6,500 years ago! (See illustration 7.) That's 1,000 years *before* the Stonehenge in England. Since the first Egyptian dynastic period began in 3400 BC with Pharaoh Hsekiu in Lower Egypt (the northern Delta area) and Pharaoh Scorpion I in Upper Egypt (the southern mountainous area), the Nabta people would have been active for roughly 3,000 years *before* the Egyptian kingdoms. The Dynastic period began in 3400 BC and ended in 525 BC when Egypt was conquered by the Persian Empire, ending the reign of the last Egyptian pharaoh, Ankhkaenre Psamtik III. You may have thought that Cleopatra VII was the last pharaoh of Egypt, but by the time she came along, true Egyptians had been ruled and assimilated by Persians and Greeks for some 500 years.

One last detail about Nabta: We know that this predynastic "Stonehenge" complex once stood on the shoreline of an ancient lake that was formed roughly in 9000 BC when the African monsoon shifted north and tropical rainfall occurred. Then, the African monsoon began to drift to the southwest around 2800 BC, and the desertification that we see today began. Today Egypt is desert on the east, south, and west, except for a little irrigated area along both banks of the Nile River and canals that run off the great river. A high culture capable of building a Stonehenge would have had lush living conditions for nearly 6,000 years, and this would have included the first 1,600 years of the pharaonic dynasties. Interestingly, this means that the Sphinx could have existed in a time of tropical conditions. It would certainly explain the running–water erosion marks on the walls of the Sphinx Pit. But that's another issue—one that we are not getting into here.

The earliest *written* papyruses of the *Egyptian Book of the Dead* date to between 1580 BC and 1350 BC, which would be the Eighteenth Dynasty—a long time after they were inscribed on early pyramid walls. However, records indicate that written copies existed as early as 2750 BC but none have been found.

No two copies of the *Egyptian Book of the Dead* contain the same text; presumably because they were produced individually by different scribes with their own and their client's prejudices. The variations in content also reflect the time period in which they were written and are categorized according to these four main editions:

1. The Heliopolitan version written in hieroglyphics and edited by the priests of the college of Annu in Heliopolis, which began during the Fifth Dynasty (2498–2345 BC). However, these priests indicate in their records that there were previous editions dating back to 2750 BC (again, none have been found—yet).

2. The Theban version, which was commonly written on papyruses in hieroglyphics and was divided into chapter–like sections, each having a distinct title but no specific order to the sections. This version was from the Eighteenth to Twentieth Dynasties (1549–1064 BC).

3. Next there was a hieroglyphic and hieratic version that was closely related to the Theban version, which also had chapters but no fixed order of chapters and was used mainly in the Twentieth Dynasty (1187–1064 BC).

4. The Säite (Greek) version was used after the Twenty–Sixth Dynasty to the end of the Ptolemaic Period. This version had chapters that were arranged in a definite order. It is commonly written in hieroglyphics and in hieratic.

Much later, in 1805 AD, Napoleon's staff created the first modern reproduction of the *Egyptian Book of the Dead*.

Of course no one could translate the *Egyptian Book of the Dead* until the discovery of the Rosetta Stone in 1799 by a French soldier, Pierre–François Bouchard, of Napoleon's expeditionary team, and then not until 1822 when Jean–François Champollions' translation of the stone was published. From 1822 on Egyptian hieroglyphs could be deciphered.

The text of the *Egyptian Book of the Dead* was originally written in both red and black ink; in some cases it was highly illustrated, in others a single illustration opened a chapter, and in the Theban editions there were no illustrations at all. Red ink was usually reserved for the titles of the chapters, opening and closing sections of the utterances, the instructions on how to perform the incantations correctly, and for important names. Black ink was used for the overall text of the manuscript. (See illustrations 8, 9, 10.)

The *Egyptian Book of the Dead* is also found on the walls of the tombs in the Valley of the Kings in the mountains across from modern–day Luxor, ancient Thebes. (See illustration 11.)

Most of the texts in the *Egyptian Book of the Dead* begin with the word *ro* and may be translated as *mouth, speech, utterance, spell, enchantment,* or *incantation*. Some archaeologists consider these sections of the *Egyptian Book of the Dead* to be spells cast to guide and protect the soul on his or her journey through the underworld to the heavens. In the first chapters the "deceased" or *initiate* enters the "tomb," descends into the "underworld," and goes through a series of incantations to awaken its abilities to speak, hear, and move through various passages required for his or her successful transition through the realms of the dead—of course we are speaking of the *living* dead. The next chapters educate the initiate about the origins of the gods or creative forces and key places. Next are chapters guiding the dead or initiate through the sky in sunlight and in the sun boat, then by night descending again into the underworld to meet Osiris, judge of the souls. Final chapters assert the person's right to be among the citizens of heaven and to be among the gods.

Here is a brief summary of the major sections of the *Egyptian Book of the Dead*:

Chapters 1–16: The deceased or initiate leaves the "House of the

Dead" and enters the tomb. It descends into the underworld. Here the soul body regains its powers of movement without physical muscles and speech without vocal cords.

Chapters 17–63: The mythic origin of the gods and secret places are explained. Then the disembodied deceased or initiate is made to live again in order for it to arise and be reborn with the morning sun—not as physical bodies but as active spirit beings.

Chapters 64–129: The deceased or initiate travels across the sky in the Boat of the Sun as one of the blessed dead. In the evening, the deceased or initiate travels to the underworld to appear before Osiris and have its heart weighed in the balance against the "feather of truth."

Chapters 130–189: Having been acknowledged and vindicated of all accusations, the deceased or initiate assumes power as one of the godlings among the gods. This section also includes assorted chapters on protective amulets, provision of "food," and important places.

As we learned in the previous chapter, in 1924 researchers and authors David Davidson and H. Aldersmith published a large book titled *The Great Pyramid: Its Divine Message*. In this book the prophecy timeline inside the Great Pyramid was meticulously detailed and correlated to passages in the *Egyptian Book of the Dead* and then to the known world events and assumed future events.

The Davidson–Aldersmith list of correlates between passageways and chambers in the Great Pyramid and terms and verses in the *Egyptian Book of the Dead* are as follows:

GREAT PYRAMID	EGYPTIAN BOOK OF THE DEAD
The Great Pyramid	"The Light" (*Ta Khut*)
The Descending Passageway	"The Descent"
The Ascending Passageway and the Grand Gallery	"Double Hall of Truth"
Entrance to Ascending Passageway	"Door of the Ascent"
Ascending Passageway	"Hall of Truth in Darkness"
Grand Gallery	"Hall of Truth in Light"
Antechamber to King's Chamber	"Chamber of the Triple Veil"

GREAT PYRAMID	EGYPTIAN BOOK OF THE DEAD
King's Chamber	"Chamber of Resurrection"
	"Chamber of the Grand Orient"
	"Chamber of the Open Tomb"
Passageway to the Queen's Chamber	"Access to Chamber of Regeneration"
Queen's Chamber	"Chamber of Regeneration"
	"Chamber of Rebirth"
	"Chamber of the Moon"
Subterranean Chamber	"Chamber of Chaos"
	"Chamber of Upside-Downness"
	"Chamber of Central Fire"
Well Shaft	"Well of Life"
Construction Chambers	"Secret Places of the Hidden God"

This chart looks quite clear, but if one were to read the *Egyptian Book of the Dead* in an effort to find these correlates, one would quickly become perplexed. For example, the "Double Hall of Truth" cannot be found in the *Egyptian Book of the Dead*. One would first have to know that the goddess Ma'at (also Maat) is the goddess of truth, and thus realize that the "Hall of Double Ma'at" is Davidson's Double Hall of Truth. Another example is Davidson's "Chamber of Upside–Downness." It cannot be found in the ancient text. However, the *Egyptian Book of the Dead* does teach how not to walk upside–down in the underworld, which Davidson then correlates to the subterranean chamber. However, in examining Davidson's research more closely, it turns out that he got many of his correlates directly from W. Marsham Adams' book, *The House of the Hidden Places*, and Adams was not always getting his information directly from the *Egyptian Book of the Dead*. For example, Adams' information about the Queen's Chamber and its correlation with the Second Birth comes from an inscription on the vase of Osur–Ur, which Adams got from Archibald Henry Sayce's (1846-1933) four volumes titled *Records of the Past* (published in 1888 and 1890). (See the Gospel of John 3:3-8 which explains that the First Birth is the birth of the physical being and that the Second Birth is the birth of the spiritual being.) Of course this does not mean that the information is not valuable and helpful to our study, but it is clearly not coming from the *Egyptian Book of the Dead*, although it is inspired by content in the *Egyptian Book of the Dead*. In this instance we learn from the inscription on the vase that Osiris is the "Second Birth, the Mystery of the Soul, Maker of the gods." We also learn that Osiris' sister Isis is the queen of the Queen's Chamber. It is she who brings the magic of rebirth, as quoted in the *Egyptian Book of the Dead*: "The Osiris [person's name here], whose word is truth, says: 'The blood of Isis, the spells of Isis, the magical powers of Isis, shall make this great one strong, and shall be an amulet of protection [for him against] that would do to him the things which he abominates.'" Utterance 156 (7, p. 43)

In Chapter 5 we will go through the *Egyptian Book of the Dead*, correlating it with passageways and chambers inside the Great Pyramid. But first we need to familiarize ourselves with the Egyptian view of the "passage" of the deceased or initiate. It is a passage from physically incarnate human being to heavenly Star-god among all the Star-gods.

4

The Passage from Human Being to Star-God

B efore we can fully understand Egyptian perspectives on the transition from physicality to spirituality, we need to realize that we are speaking about the *ancient* Egyptians, not the modern Arab Egyptians who have a much different view of life, one based on Islamic and Arabian traditions. Although they have ruled Egypt for nearly 1,400 years, they do not hold any of the ancient Egyptian's views.

Mohammed lived from April 26, 570 to June 8, 632, and Muslim Arabs invaded Egypt in 642 AD, long after the ancient Egyptians had been conquered many times and assimilated into many cultures. If we overlook the brief and limited rule by Hyksos raiders, merchants, and migrants from across the Red Sea (1620–1530 BC) who controlled only the Eastern Nile Delta region and ruled a population consisting largely of Syrian–Palestinian migrants and soldiers and if we accept that the Nubian invasion in 1075 BC simply merged two cultures (Nubian and Egyptian) who were practically indistinguishable from one another by virtue of Egypt's rule of Nubia (Kush) for nearly five hundred years (1550–1080 BC), then ancient Egypt really did not lose its unique cultural views until the Persians began invading in 525 BC. The Persian invasions basically ended *ancient* Egyptian sovereignty. The Persian invasions were followed by the Greek invasion in 332 BC, then the Roman invasion in 30 BC, and then, when the Roman Empire was divided, sovereignty over Egypt shifted to the Byzantine Empire in 395 AD, and finally the Muslim–Arab invasion in 642 AD, which began the *Fatimid Dynasty*, an Islamic dynasty. And their descendants continue to govern Egypt today as the Islamic Arab Republic of Egypt.

Let's not include the people who built the Nabta Playa "stonehenge," which would extend the beginning of this culture back closer to 9560 BC, because they were not well known by the Egyptians who subsequently wrote about them. With all of this in mind, we are looking at the views of a people who lived along the Nile River from roughly 4000 BC (predynastic) to 525 BC (the Persian invasion). These are the ancient Egyptians in the context of this information.

Ancient Egyptian Perspectives

In the *Egyptian Book of the Dead*, the existence of the deceased or initiate began long before its incarnation into this world. But the passage of the entity from this world to the next is from its human incarnation, through the transition of physical death, on through many transcending experiences and tests, until it reaches its ultimate potential: a fully conscious and eternal Star-god in the infinite heavens, living among the other light beings of creation. In the *Egyptian Book of the Dead* the deceased or initiate *asserts* that he or she was originally conceived in the primordial "sea" of infinity by the self-created god-of-all-gods Atum (also written Tem). The following creation myth is found in the pyramid text of the *Egyptian Book of the Dead* on the walls of Pepi I's pyramid:

The story begins with a *creative essence* appearing out of the infinite, dark nothingness—willing itself into being. This essence evolved into a creator called *Atum* (also known as *Atem* and *Tem*, in Wallis Budge's translation of the *Egyptian Book of the Dead* he uses Tem). This name means the "Complete One." Within the Complete One was his shadow, which was the infinite womb of mother *Iusaaset* (pronounced *e-oo-sa–ah-set*; meaning "mother of the first gods" but also "grandmother of the subsequent gods"). The two of them—the self–created Atum and the unseen Iusaaset—conceived *breath* and *moisture*. Sadly, these two offspring became lost in the infinite chaos of dark nothingness; therefore Atum conceived of the conceiver of Light (Ra). The Light was born inside the dark chaos. Atum sent the Eye of Light that penetrates the darkness to find the lost primordial children. The Eye of Light was Ra. When Ra rose from the hidden depths of the primordial sea, he immediately gave life to Ma'at, "Truth." Ancient Egyptians believed that the creation we know could not have come into existence until Truth (Ma'at) first established order, balance, and harmony. The Egyptians believed that if Truth (Ma'at) had not been conceived, then chaos would have reigned and the primordial sea would have reclaimed the manifested universe into her unseen depths. With order established, and upon finding the lost children, Atum, who was now united with Ra, was now called Atum Ra (see illustration 12), he then named Breath *life*, and Moisture *order*. Then, Atum Ra bound Life and Order together and with these two now united, he made *air* (the Egyptian god *Shu*) and *mist* (*Tefnut*). Then, by kissing his daughter Mist, Atum Ra created the first mound (firmament) in the primordial sea, which was the Ben–ben Mound. Like the Mayan legend of the celestial turtle rising from out of the infinite primordial sea, the Ben–ben Mound rose from out of the vast expanse of the motionless sea of the infinite depths. Then Atum Ra rested on the mound, while *life-air* (Shu) and *order-mist* (Tefnut) mated to create *earth* (the god *Geb*) and *sky* (the goddess *Nut*, pronounced *noot*, rhymes with *toot*). Earth and Sky then conceived five more godlings: *Osiris*, god of fertility, resurrection, and judge of the heart of every soul; *Isis*, goddess of magic, motherhood, and "Mother of the Universe"; *Set*, god of chaos, confusion, storms, wind, the desert, and foreign lands; *Nephthys*, "Mistress of the House," "Friend of the Dead," and goddess of divine help and protection; and *Horus the Elder*, god of light, whose left eye was the sun and right eye the moon. (See illustration 13.)

In this creation story we see the original chaos of "dark nothingness" and then the subsequent personification of chaos in the god "Set." In the *Egyptian Book of the Dead*, there is "the day of the combat of the Two Fighters"; these were none other than Set and Horus with Set being the chaos and Horus being the light. During these times there was an upside-downness, evil reigned over goodness, symbolized by Set's victory over Osiris, in which goodness was scattered to the four winds by Set's dismembering of Osiris' body; thus no one could see the full nature of the goodness and stability that perfect Osiris represented.

In this story we also learn how the Egyptians believed that everything had a balancing counterpart: the infinite darkness had the Eye of Light, chaos had *truth* that brought order, balance, and harmony, and the infinite void now had a *place* within it in the form of the mound or firmament.

In the *Egyptian Book of the Dead* the deceased or initiate asserts his or her personal identity with these primordial gods, even to the point of using their names for his or her own name, such as Osiris Ani and Horus Ani. Each entity came from out of the heavens and the godlings of the heavens, and each returns to them when the physical incarnation ends.

(The *ancient* Egyptians did not consider death a cessation of life. For them it was only a transition from one form of life to another.)

The Passage from Human Being to Star-god

An ancient Egyptian did not consider him- or herself to be simply a body with a personality, as many do today. A whole human being was much more complex. Each incarnate entity was composed of a physical body (*ha*, roughly meaning "flesh" and "that which decays"; also *khat*, meaning "body," but also an "animal's belly"); a soul (*ba*) with a soul body (*sahu*, which is the soul's metaphysical vessel while the body is said to be its physical "garment"); a "life force" that is also the spirit double of the physical person (*ka*); a *metaphysical* heart (*ab*, also spelled *ib* or *jb*), a shadow (*sheut*, also spelled *shut* and *swt*, and also termed the *khaibit*); an energy or power (*sekhem*); a specific name (*ren*); and finally, a celestial Star-god (*akhu*, also *akh* and *khu*) with its "Star-body" (*khab*, the godling's vessel).

Physical Body (ha/khat)

Soul and Soul Body (ba and sahu)
Life Force/Spirit Double (ka)
Metaphysical Heart (ab)
Shadow (sheut or khaibit)
Power and Name (sekhem and ren)
Star-god and Star-body (akhu and khab)

The ancient Egyptians believed that the physical body died when the life force and spirit double (ka) left their carnal abode (ha/khat). After death much of the entity lived on—*actively so*—as a disembodied being. It made many transitions from earthy consciousness and existence to heavenly, even to the level of a "Star-god" (akhu).

Curiously, the Maya, Toltec, and Aztec cultures have similar tale in which the "Children of God" put their celestial hearts into the "sacred fire" in order to bring more light upon the Earth as they battle with the Lords of the Underworld. The new lights in the darkness are these stars, and each of these stars is a specific heart from one of the Children. Once they are victorious, they will reclaim their star-hearts.

Since the *Egyptian Book of the Dead* describes the passage from human being to Star-god, let's explore the parts of being a bit further before we correlate the *Egyptian Book of the Dead* with the passageways and chambers in the Great Pyramid.

The Body (ha/khat)

The ancient Egyptian considered his or her physical body to be a most precious vehicle for living in this realm of matter with three dimensions, and yet the body was also a well-designed temple for carrying the *metaphysical* elements of one's complete being. However, human physical bodies were still evolving, so a beautiful, healthy body was an object of worship in ancient Egypt. Everyone beautified their bodies and kept them as healthy as possible. Bathing, perfuming, dressing with linen, gold, jewelry, wigs, and headdresses were all considered to be ideal, even for men. Beauty and health were honored. Of course, the one exception was the brief seventeen-year reign of Akhenaten (1353–1336 BC), who did not stylize his appearance toward beauty and health—

at least not toward the beauty that was standard in those times. Yet, despite his personal presentations, Akhenaten had one of the most beautiful wives in all of Egyptian history, and he proudly had her depicted by his artists. She was the famous *Nefertiti*, originally pronounced *Naf-teta*, meaning, "The beauty has come." The bust of this woman is among the most famous artifacts in all of ancient Egypt's treasures. Tut's golden funerary mask is likely the most famous. (See illustrations 14 and 15.)

(When the dead body becomes a mummy, it is no longer a dead, decaying corpse but is now a magical instrument for assisting afterlife conditions) Even so, attempts to preserve the body after death did not become important until the Fourth Dynasty (2613–2498 BC); and full preservation or true *mummification* did not fully develop until the Middle Kingdom and was not perfected until the Eighteenth Dynasty (1549–1292 BC). Surprisingly, after this amazing achievement, the quality of mummification *declined* to the point that during the Ptolemaic period it was mostly decorating the corpse rather than preserving it. This is an indication that the ancient wisdom was slipping away as the culture became more earthly oriented and materially inclined, losing its spiritual awareness and heavenly afterlife orientation. The physical life became more important than the celestial life—and this was a most dramatic though gradual shift in consciousness and philosophy for the Egyptians.

Why mummify the physical body if the soul and spirit and the afterlife are more important? Despite what some teach, resurrection in ancient Egypt was more about becoming alive after death than about raising the dead body to live in some form in the metaphysical realms or even on the earth. Mummification was perfected because the ancient priests and priestesses, and likely the better-educated people, knew that the soul (ba) and the life force/spirit double (ka) were so integrated into the physical body during incarnation that there remained a subtle but significant *connection* between them. Therefore, the physical could be put into a condition that would allow the soul and spirit twin to better prepare its life beyond incarnation.

Here's an utterance from the *Egyptian Book of the Dead* that reveals how influential one may be while the mummy is in the tomb: "Hail, O ye Doorkeepers, I have completed my journey. I am like unto you. I have come forth by day. I have advanced on my legs. I have gained the master over my footsteps. Hail, ye Spirit-souls! I, even I, do know the hidden roads and the Gates of Sekhet Aaru [a place with heavenly fields of *rushes*, which are a family of flowering plants that resemble grasses]. I live there. Verily, I, even I, have come, I have overthrown my enemies upon the earth, although my body lies a mummy in the tomb." Utterance 86 (5, p. 521)

It was also believed that the soul and spirit twin occasionally returned to the physical body after death, thus magical words (*hekau*) and sacred rituals were used around the physical body to fully reinvigorate the soul for metaphysical consciousness and activity. Amulets, papyruses, and texts in stone were placed on or near the mummy; prayers, hymns, and spells were spoken to it; all in an effort to affect the visiting soul and spirit double. The ceremony of the "Opening the Mouth" is an example of a preparation for speaking in the metaphysical realms when one no longer had physical vocal cords. (See illustration 16.) Here is an "utterance" from the *Egyptian Book of the Dead* concerning the Opening of the Mouth: "Grant you to me my mouth that I may speak therewith, and cause sepulchral offerings to be made to me in your presence." Utterance 72 (5, p. 370)

The words of power and the rituals also helped fully *release* the soul body (sahu) from its entanglement in the physical body during its incarnation, allowing it to better function in nonphysical realms.

During incarnation the physical body was indeed the temple of the soul and spirit, and after death the mummy was an instrument of assistance for releasing the soul's and spirit twin's attachment to the physical body.

Soul and Soul Body (ba and sahu)

When the ancient Egyptians looked around for some image in this world that could convey the soul, they decided to use a bird's body with a human head. (See illustration 17.) The soul was everything about a person that made him or her an individual in all realms of life, physical and metaphysical, yet since it survived this physical life, a bird's body symbolized the ability to fly high above earth life. The soul's vessel (sahu) is an incorruptible "body" used during discarnate sojourns. It arises from the material body. Today we might correlate the etheric body with the soul's vessel and the astral body with the akhu's vessel (khab). At death the human-headed bird would spread his or her wings and lift out of the physical body holding the *shen* ring in its bird feet. The shen is the icon of a circle wrapped tightly to a shaft, symbolizing eternity (the circle) and temporality (the shaft), as well as the yin (circle) and yang (shaft); both are innate qualities of the soul. (See illustration 18.) The outer self may display one gender, but the soul self contained both yin and yang. The soul was considered to be actively dynamic in the metaphysical dimensions of the underworld and the heavens. Upon physical death the soul (ba) would seek out the spirit twin (ka) to unite with it and thereby create the celestial self (akhu).

In the *Egyptian Book of the Dead* we find this passage: "The road of souls is opened. My twin soul sees the Great God in the Boat of Rà, on the day of souls. My soul is in the front thereof with the counter of the years. Come, the Eye of Horus has delivered for me my soul, my ornaments are established on the brow of Ra. Light is on the faces of those who are in the members of Osiris [the dead]. You shall not hold captive my soul." Utterance 92 (5, p. 475)

Life Force and Spirit Twin (ka)

The ka is akin to *energy* in the sense that energy is the essence of matter; also, it is the energy "twin" of the physical person.

The determining difference between a live person and a dead one was the presence or absence of the life force (ka). This is the *ch'i* or *qi*, and the *prâna* of Asian cultures, the Greek philosopher Posidonius' "vital force" (ca 135–51 BC), the *entelécheia* of Aristotle, the German philosopher Schopenhauer's "will-to-live," the *élan vital* that was first coined by French philosopher Henri Bergson in his 1907 book *Creative Evolution*, and the Judeo-Christian concept of *spirit* as the breath of life (Latin *spiritus*, meaning "breath," and Hebrew *ruach*, meaning "breath"); as in "The Lord God formed man of dust from the ground, and breathed into his nostrils the breath of life; and man became a living being." (Genesis 2:7 RSV)

In addition to the concept of the life force, ka also means the "twin" or "double." The ka was depicted with bright eyes and a shadowy replica of the human body. It was believed that this spirit double lived inside each person, and when it left, death resulted. It could be considered to be the life-energy field of the person and what gave life to the physical body. It is a personal life force that is in all living beings. It can be seen as the *vitality* of the being. It is also seen in the feelings, emotions, and passion of a person.

The Egyptian glyph for the ka is a pair of shoulders with raised arms (thus *twins* or the *double*) in the position of adoration of the divine, but with no head between the arms—conveying that it is that inspiring *feeling* one has when in divine adoration but not thinking or consciousness.

An ancient Egyptian who was dying was said to be "going to his ka." A discarnate being was said to be living *in* his or her ka.

Curiously, the ka could die too. This was known as the "second death" and was to be avoided because it meant the complete extinction of that being. Offerings, prayers, hymns, and spells could help ensure the existence of the entity. The ka could temporarily inhabit a statue near the corpse and would do so if it was provided a properly prepared statue in a secure ka chapel. But once the body decomposed, the ka was likely to move on beyond physicality.

(The ka of a dead person could affect earthly life and those in earthly life, similar to the beliefs about deceased ancestors influencing incarnate family members and their life circumstances. Each of the Egyptian gods had its unique ka. For example, the ka guardian of the pyramids was none other than Osiris.)

The Heart (*ab*)

The ancient Egyptians believed that thought, reason, motivation, free will, and will power came from the metaphysical heart, not from the organic brain or earthly personality. In fact, the heart determined how one's afterlife was going to be. The deceased or initiate would be led to the weighing scales of a judgment hall, and his or her metaphysical heart would be placed on one half of a scale while the feather of truth was on the opposite half. If the heart was lighter than the feather, then the Egyptian could journey into the afterlife realms. However, if the heart was heavier than the feather, then a specific beast gobbled up the heavy heart. In this way the metaphysical heart is also associated with *conscience*. A heart weighed down with regret, unfulfilled desires, possessive earthly appetites, and too much of the material life would not be light enough to allow the deceased or the initiate to lift up into the heavens.

On the walls of the pyramid of Unas we find this passage concerning the heart and its influence upon the ka and ba: "I will be in the sky, a command shall be made for my benefit in Memphis, I shall be aware in my heart, I shall have power in my heart, I shall have power in my arms, I shall have power in my legs, I shall have power to do whatsoever my ka pleases, and my ba will not be fettered at the gates of the West [death] when I go in or out in peace." Utterance 26

The Shadow (sheut or khaibit)

The shadow was considered to be a living, essential part of an individual. The shadow had power and could move fast. Everything in Egyptian thought existed in duality, in its complementary condition or form. Also, every thing and every being were always intertwined with the universe. Everyone has a shadow. The shadow is always present. It is an integral part of the whole of a person. The ancient Egyptians depicted the shadow in humanlike form but totally black, with no detailed features. Unlike Jungian psychology, the Egyptian shadow was not considered to carry unconscious or repressed weaknesses, shortcomings, and instincts. Rather, it was simply unseen aspects of the whole entity. It did not influence instinctively or irrationally. Alive or dead, a person always has his or her shadow. And a shadow cannot exist without its associated entity. (See illustration 17b.)

In the *Egyptian Book of the Dead* we have these passages: "You shall not keep imprisoned my shadow. The way is open to my soul and to my shadow;" Utterance 92 and, "If this Chapter be known by the deceased he shall be able to transform himself into a Spirit-Soul who shall be equipped with his soul and his shadow in the Divine Netherworld (*Khert-*

Neter), and he shall not be shut up inside any door to the Entrance to the Netherworld (*Amentet*), when he is coming forth upon the Earth or when he is going back into Divine Netherworld (*Khert-Neter*)." Utterance 155

The Power and Name(sekhem and ren)

The sound of the name was the perfect expression of the being, and each being had its unique name/sound. In the theology of Memphis, Egypt, it is taught that the creator god Ptah brought the entire cosmos into existence by uttering the names of all things and beings. One's true or vital name was the key to that one's existence among the multitude. The true name needed to be protected, to be maintained, and to be known to the entity and others among the multitude of realms of life, physical and metaphysical. If others learned the true name, they could use it for power and influence. If one's name stopped being thought or spoken, then one no longer existed, slipping back into the primordial sea from which all life manifested.

In the Coffin Texts, spell number 572, we have this statement: "I know my name, I am not ignorant of it, I will be among those that follow after Osiris . . . "(16) Osiris is the example of how to die, resurrect, and live in the realms beyond physical life. He also happens to be the judge of everyone who comes over to the other side from this world.

The Egyptian Book of the Dead opens with this utterance to Osiris and Isis: "Homage to thee, Osiris, Lord of eternity, King of the Gods, whose names are manifold, whose forms are holy, thou being of hidden form in the temples, whose Ka is holy. . . . Thou art Atum (Tem), the feeder of Kau (plural of Ka), the Governor of the Companies of the gods. Thou art the beneficent Spirit among the spirits. . . . The Companies of the Gods praise thee, and the gods of the Netherworld (Duat) smell the earth in paying homage to thee. The uttermost parts of the earth bow before thee, and the limits of the skies entreat thee with supplications when they see thee. The holy ones are overcome before thee, and all Egypt offers thanksgiving unto thee when it meets Thy Majesty. Thou art a shining Spirit–Body, the governor of Spirit–Bodies; permanent is thy rank, established is thy rule. Thou art the well–doing Power (Sekhem) of the Company of the Gods, gracious is thy face, and beloved by him that sees it. Thy fear is set in all the lands by reason of thy perfect love, and they cry out to thy name making it the first of names, and all people make offerings to thee. Thou art the lord who art commemorated in heaven and upon earth. . . . [Your] sister Isis has protected you, and has repulsed the fiends, and turned aside calamities (of evil). She uttered the spell with the magical power of her mouth. Her tongue was perfect, and it never halted at a word. Beneficent in command and word was Isis, the woman of magical spells, the advocate of her brother. She sought him untiringly, she wandered round and round about this earth in sorrow, and she alighted not without finding him. She made light with her feathers, she created air with her wings, and she uttered the death wail for her brother. She raised up the inactive members of whose heart was still, she drew from him his essence [life-giving mystical "sperm"], she made an heir [Horus, the redeemer], she reared the child in loneliness, and the place where he was not known, and he grew in strength and stature, and his hand was mighty in the House of Geb (the house in the Earth, which is his physical body). The Company of the Gods rejoiced, rejoiced, at the coming of Horus, the son of Osiris, whose heart was firm, the triumphant, the son of Isis, the heir of Osiris."

Names were powerfully important for they literally opened gates and subdued challenges. From the *Egyptian Book of the Dead*: "I know you, and I know your names, and I know also the name of the mighty god before whose face you set your celestial food." Utterance 72

Knowing a name was tantamount to knowing the power sounds that opened the way for one to participate in higher and higher levels of the afterlife, and it overcame the power of the forces against oneself.

Star-god and Star-body

The Star–god is the magical, radiant, most essential portion of one's being. It lives among the stars and was, in fact, a specific star. It unites with the gods, lives among them, imperishable. In order for this star-light being to come alive, one's soul (ba) and spirit twin (ka) must unite. This union required many carefully executed steps to be taken and many tests to be overcome, but when the union occurred, the akhu was magically liberated and alive forever. The akhu may be thought of as a

"Star-god," a divine being among the major gods of heaven and within the infinite essence of the Great Life Force, or Great Ka. Here are two passages from the *Egyptian Book of the Dead*: "Thou shall come forth into heaven, thou shall sail over the sky, and thou shall hold loving intercourse with the Star-gods"; and, "Homage to you, O you gods of the Netherworld (Duat), whose faces are turned back, whose powers advance, conduct you me to the Star-gods which never rest." Utterance 78

The Star-god travels in a star body called the khab, it's radiance is visible throughout the universe.

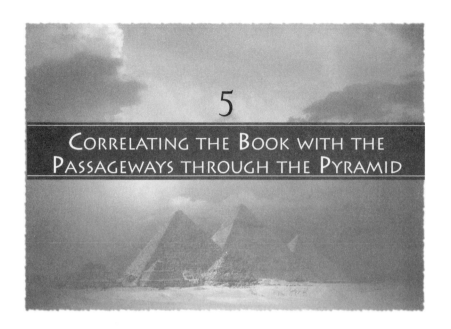

5

CORRELATING THE BOOK WITH THE PASSAGEWAYS THROUGH THE PYRAMID

A lthough the *Egyptian Book of the Dead* is considered to be a guide and a spell-casting protective charm for a discarnate person, in this context it must also be such for an *incarnate* person receiving training about death, the afterlife, and the important "places," challenges, and transitions experienced as one moves from physical activity and consciousness to *metaphysical* activity and awareness. And since there were no mummies or even evidence of mummies found in any of the major pyramids in Egypt, this idea of training and initiation is not as farfetched as it may first appear. Add to this that even the ancient Egyptians considered it important to know the *Egyptian Book of the Dead* while incarnate, as seen in this passage: "If this text be known upon earth . . . then will he be able to come forth on any day he please, and to enter into his [afterlife] habitation unobstructed." (*Papyrus of Ani*) (5, p. 147)

With the possible exception of the Tibetans and their *Tibetan Book of the Dead* (which was written ca 8 AD, long after ancient Egypt was history)-there has been no culture on this planet as interested in and as attentive to the afterlife more than the ancient Egyptians—not even hellfire-and-brimstone, fear-generating Christian priests and preachers had as much detail about the afterlife or redemptive tips and techniques for the dead as the Egyptians did.

Notes of Interest

Keep in mind that there are several editions of the *Egyptian Book of the Dead*, some with chapters and some without them, some have texts that others do not. The following correlation uses the chapter structure of the Säite edition with the text of the Theban edition. The Theban edition is used because of its antiquity, believing that the older versions more closely represent the original text. However, there are sections that appear in the Säite edition that are not in the Theban edition, and they relate well to the Great Pyramid, so these passages are included, stating the belief that the initiations in this pyramid continued through many dynasties. These inclusions are indicated in brackets. Additionally, if the Egyptian word or name has some significance, then it is included in brackets, as well as any spelling variations of which there are many.

Also, in the text there are many *foreshadowing* statements of events to come and achievements to be realized by the deceased and initiate. Often these appear in the text long before one ever reaches the opportunities or places—likely preparing the deceased or initiate for what is to come. There are also *cycles* to the deceased's or initiate's passage—the journey does not proceed in a straight line but returns to previous locations, challenges, godly influences, and activities to perhaps reinforce that gained from the first encounter with these.

Correlating the *Book* with the Passageways and Chambers

A correlation of the journey through the chapter-like sections in the *Egyptian Book of the Dead* with the passageways and chambers in the Great Pyramid would go something like the following:

Entering the Tomb and the Underworld
Chapter 1–4 [3 and 4 are from the Säite edition]:

With many praises of the gods and the sacred places, and self-identification with the gods and one's rightful belonging in the sacred places, the journey of the deceased or initiate begins with his or her soul body [*sahu*] moving in a procession from the "House of the Dead" [possibly the Great Pyramid's Mortuary Temple] to the tomb [the Great Pyramid] and to the entrance to the underworld [*Amentet*—meaning the place where the sun sets and is associated with the original entrance into the Great Pyramid].

Here the Captain of the Soldiers, who guards the entrance, is honored, and the soul body of the deceased or initiate descends into the underworld or netherworld [*Duat, Tuat, Tuaut*]—which would be equivalent to entering the Great Pyramid and moving down the long descending passageway to the subterranean chamber (often called "the pit.") This chamber is deep in the bedrock of the Giza Plateau *beneath* the Great Pyramid. Another name for this location is *Neter-khert*, which literally means, "divine [*neter*] subterranean place [*khert* and *khertet*]," which fits perfectly with the location and nature of the pit. In these sections the deceased or initiate is also instructed to wake up and be alive in the underworld

Chapters 5–6—Still in the subterranean chamber of the Great Pyramid:

Now the speakers of the text are instructing the deceased or initiate that he or she is not allowed to do work in the underworld but can energize inanimate objects to do the work. These objects are called *ushabtiu* figurines. They were made of stone, alabaster, wood, clay, or glazed faience. They were in the form of the god Osiris as a mummy. They were placed in wooden boxes in the tomb, laid along the floor of the tomb, and sometimes placed inside the coffin. Ushabtiu figures were used to perform work for the deceased or initiate, who is considered to be condemned to "sow the fields, fill the canals with water, and carry sand from the West (land of the dead) to the East (land of the living)."

Chapters 7–14 [Chapter 11 is from the Säite edition]—still in the subterranean chamber:

Now the initiate meets the enemies of anyone who seeks to move up into the heavens. These enemies challenge him. He must spear the head of the poisonous, ankle-biting snake *Apep* [also *Apepi*]. He must also honor helpful influences by bending his knee before them. One such is more of a symbolic icon: it is a staff with a ram's head on top and on the ram's head is a raised cobra—emblems of having a strongheaded mind and a raised kundalini life force. In this phase of death or initiation, he must drive away "shame" from his heart if he is to ascend into the higher, more heavenly realms.

Chapters 15–20 [Chapter 19 is from the Säite edition]—ascending out of the subterranean chamber through "secret places" to the first ascending passageway:

This begins with a hymn of praise to Ra when he rises in the eastern horizon of heaven. It continues with Ra rising in the "land of the living" and the land of *Amentet* (also *Ament, Amentit, Imentet, Imentit*). As we saw in chapter one, Amentet is the name for the entrance to the netherworld. But it is also the name of the goddess friend of the dead, and the personification of the Land of the West, *amenty* and *imnty*, the land of the setting sun. It was Amentet who welcomed the deceased to their new dwelling place in the netherworld. She was also a goddess who helped with the rebirthing process of the spirit body, who regenerated the deceased with metaphysical food and water. Thus she may also be associated with the Queen's Chamber of the "second birth" in the Great Pyramid—and we may now be in the Queen's Chamber.

(From other Egyptian sources we know that this chamber is also associated with Isis, the sister-spouse of Osiris. She was called "The Queen" or "Mistress of the Pyramid," and it was her tears at the death of Osiris that brought the flooding by the Nile to fertilize the land with rich silt and her sunshine at Osiris' rebirth that brought light and life to the fields. As we quoted earlier, it was her blood, magic, and power that gave power and new life to the initiate or deceased.)

In these chapters we have, in addition, the worship of the sun by mythological beings, as well as worshipping and honoring the "beautiful" land of the living dead, which is the horizon of the *setting* sun in this world. Of course, the sun never really sets; it simply makes a journey through the underworld until it rises again on the eastern horizon.

Here, too, we have the beginning of the transformations into other pleasing forms.

Chapters 21–30 [Chapter 21 is from the Säite edition]—still in the Queen's Chamber:

From here the entity is guided to regain its powers of movement and speech, even though the physical legs and vocal cords are dead or as if dead.

The initiate has ascended out of the pit through the first ascending passageway. And as the entity ascended, powers are being regained, and the entity is taught the origins of the gods (which may be considered as macrocosmic and microcosmic archetypes of influences affecting each person's energies and abilities) and the "places" (or states of consciousness and awareness). Here we have now entered the Chamber of Rebirth (the Queen's Chamber). As these truths are comprehended and become a portion of the entity's vibrations and mental construct, he or she is "psyched" into coming alive again, being reborn, and rising like the morning sun. These words are spoken aloud: "I live . . . I live."

Now the deceased or initiate is assisted into recalling his or her name (*ren*). Once the name is recalled, a new heart is given to the person. Now follow several chapters about the heart, including lessons on how not to allow one's heart to be taken from him or carried away or driven away or struck with a knife. The person's heart is honored. It is symbolized with a carnelian stone. It is presented to a trinity of gods. And ultimately it is weighed in the balance against goddess Ma'at's feather of truth. If it is lighter than the feather, the deceased or initiate is found worthy.

Now here is where a controversy develops over reincarnation, which most Egyptologists do not accept as part of the Egyptian philosophy. If the entity's heart is heavy, say from guilt or regret or unfulfilled desires (as the Buddha taught), then the little beastly god *Ammut* "The Devourer" (a composite animal with the head of a crocodile, the front legs and body of lion or leopard, and the back legs of a hippopotamus) would eat the heart. Now most Egyptologists believe that the entity then ceased to exist, and this was the "second death," as spoken of in several texts (and, interestingly, in the Christian Revelation). However, another view is that the entity would then have to reincarnate and live a life that created a lighter heart—one without guilt, regret, or heavily possessing desires. Then when the entity came before Ma'at's scales, his or her heart would be found to be lighter than the feather of Truth, and it could finally break the cycle of incarnations and ascend into the realms of heaven.

Chapters 31–51 [Chapter 49 is from the Säite edition]—leaving the Queen's Chamber and descending to the pit again:

These chapters have to do with repulsing demons, not having to go into the divine "block" a second time, and not having to walk upside-down in the underworld. These passages may indicate a return through the first ascending passageway, passed the granite plug ("the block" in chapter 40) and descending to the pit. Crocodiles, snakes, worms, beetles, and turtles must all be faced and not allowed to harm or eat the deceased or initiate and his new heart. The deceased or initiate must put an end to the wounding of his eyes in the underworld and not allow his head to be cut off.

And it is here where the greatest danger is faced: dying a second time. This second death is truly the death of self. The first death was the body, the temple of the living being, but this second death is the death of the being. It must be avoided. Even so, one must face his or her enemies and conquer them.

Now comes the strange teaching of not going into the "divine block" a second time. At this point the person is likely to be at the transitional place of the granite plug between the descending passageway and the first ascending passageway. As a physical body, one cannot go through this block, but as a spirit body, one can. However, it is now seen as something not to do again. Perhaps it indicates that once we are on the other side of this block, in the first ascending passageway, we never, ever want to descend again. Therefore, do not go into the divine block between the upper realms and the lower realms of the netherworld.

Chapters 52–62 [Chapters 52 and 58 from the Säite edition]— we are now in the Grand Gallery:

Here begins the training about neither eating (assimilating into one's heart and soul) filth nor drinking polluted water. One is taught the power to purify the water of the underworld. One is taught how to sniff the air of the netherworld. A sail is held in the deceased's or initiate's hand and up to his or her nose. One must inhale the air in this sail. One must sail up the many rivers of the netherworld with the air of these realms in one's "sail," gaining power as one does this. Finally, one is able to drink the pure water of the netherworld.

Chapters 63–107—still at the beginning of the Grand Gallery:

These chapters open with a picture of a female deceased or initiate holding a lotus and her soul, while drinking of the water of life and the trees of life are bending toward her. (See illustration 19.) The deceased or initiate is taught how not to be burned in the fire (of the spirit) or the boiling water (spirit-filled life). We see the person standing between two flames. Here begins another round of coming forth in the light or by the day, and honoring Ra. The person also honors *Meh-urt*, who is the goddess that represents the spiritual river of heaven and the ocean water where life began.

In these chapters the disembodied being is "passing through the halls of the tomb," which correlates to the two great halls in the Great Pyramid.

Here again begin a series of transformations that the deceased or initiate must learn to do at will. He or she is allowed to transform into whatever image is pleasing. After which, the person must turn into a Golden Hawk and then a Divine Hawk. After that, the person changes into a god and sends light into the darkness. Then he or she must turn into a lily, a phoenix, a heron, the serpent *Sa-Ta* (meaning, "son of the earth," and is a serpent that regenerates himself each day), a crocodile, and so on.

Now there comes a series of most important activities to be accomplished in the afterlife and likely coming to the upper levels in the Grand Gallery and the "Great Step": the reconnection of the soul (ba) to aspects of its whole being and its functionality as a spirit being. Here, too, the entity draws near to the god Thoth, author of the *Egyptian Book of the Dead* and scribe of heaven and the records on all souls. Here also the soul receives the instruments for writing his or her "Book of Life," and a boat with which to travel the realms of the heavens. He or she is trained not to sail East through the netherworld (back toward physicality and form, the land of the rising sun, and the incarnate living).

Most important of all these activities is the uniting of one's soul (ba) with one's spirit (ka), and thereby producing the *ahku* (magically influential star-self).

Chapters 108–114—still moving through the Grand Gallery, possibly even recycling through lower levels within the Gallery:

At this stage of the passage the deceased or initiate begins to know the souls of the netherworld and entering the "Fields of Peace" and the "Fields of Reeds." Here also the person is active in the Grand Gallery, known in the *Egyptian Book of the Dead* as the "Hall of Maat," the "hall of the tomb," and the "great house of the tomb." Here, in the presence of the gods, Ma'at *(Maat, Maati)* separates the entity from his or her sins, which assist the entity in seeing the "great God, the Lord of Humankind." Again the entity's heart is weighed in the balance. Now words are spoken in praise of the chiefs of judgment and the gods of the netherworld.

Chapters 115–186 [Chapters 115 and 131 are from the Säite edition]—*The End*:

The picture here is of three ibis–headed gods, the icon of Thoth, and this may indicate the entrance in the antechamber to the King's Chamber that has the chamber of the triple veils. Now the entity passes from the halls of the tomb into the "city of the sun" *(Annu)*.

The entity also meets three gods: *Thoth, Sau* [likely *Horus*], and *Atem (Tem, Tmu)*. These three may be associated with the triple veils, even the Christian and Hindu trinities: Father (Atem and Brahma), Son (Horus and Vishnu), and Holy Spirit (Thoth and Shiva). If so, they also represent a transition or integration of creator, created, and united spirit of oneness (no longer are the creator and created seen as separate).

Now the entity has a powerful staff that assists him or her in ascending the western hills, thus traveling over the netherworld and the land of the setting sun on toward the heavens. The main corridor through the netherworld is called Re–stau, and now the entity is "coming forth from the Re–stau," indicating the end of the journey.

Now there comes the chapter of "going into the great house," which is likely the King's Chamber. Here the entity stands before his or her tomb, which is likely the sarcophagus. Keep in mind the sarcophagus inside the King's Chamber has no lid and never had one. Thus, it was not meant to seal in a mummy, rather to allow an initiate to experience a deathlike transition. In these chapters the entity enters "heaven," makes perfect its ahku (magically influential star–being), and traverses the heavens with Ra and other deities. The imagery of fire is found in several of these chapters, likely symbolizing the spirit of the sacred or holy spirit. The entity comes before seven pylons. These could be the seven chakras and the seven stone layers above the King's Chamber, five from granite and two from limestone. The two limestone levels form the vaulted roof.

Now come several doors or gates through which the entity must pass, each guarded by a god. In Chapter 151 the entity meets the god Anubis (*Anpu*), who, along with Thoth, frees him or her from physicality in order to traverse the heavens. In this chapter we find the concept of "the dweller in the sepulchral chamber," indicating that we are indeed in the King's Chamber.

Chapters 155 through 160 convey a series of symbolic power gifts and amulets being given to the freed ahku (magically influential star–being): gold, amethyst, and mother–of–emerald. Eventually, Thoth opens the doors or gates of heaven. The ahku body is decorated and eventually arrives at a heavenly port. The entity is no longer an unseen spirit body. It learns to make the new body germinate and to know unmoving contentment through the water of heaven.

In Chapter 170 the entity arrives at "the roof of the offering chamber." Could this be the vaulted roof above the King's Chamber? In Chapter 175 the Star–god (ahku) comes forth from the gates of heaven and does not die a second time. He now lives in the netherworld and heaven as a citizen. In Chapter 178 we find the raising up of the spirit body, the making the eyes to see, the ears to hear, the setting of the head firmly, and the giving of powers to the spirit body.

As the *Egyptian Book of the Dead* draws to a conclusion, we have praises to Osiris and the establishment of the Osiris backbone (*Djed*), which is symbolic of a stable, enduring life.

Note: In *Egyptian Hieroglyphic Dictionary*, vol. 2, p. 913, Sir Wallis Budge writes that the Djed is the oldest symbol of Osiris, and it symbolizes his backbone and his body. Budge states that originally Osiris probably had no other body or form than the Djed. (See illustration 21.) Budge writes that the Djed hieroglyph means: "to be stable, to be permanent, abiding, established firmly, enduring." This is that unmoving content-ment that fills the heavenly being or in Christianity that "peace of God, which passes all understanding."

6
THE PROPHETIC TIMELINE DATES

I n this chapter we will examine Davidson's diagram of the Great Pyramid, his measurements, and the relationship of historical events to the timeline prophecy. However, we will do so without Davidson's obvious intention of making all the details fit with Judeo-Christian theology, and by ignoring his description of the Egyptian concepts as "spurious." Piazzi Smyth had a similar attitude toward the master builders of the amazing edifice and the authors of the *Egyptian Book of the Dead*, writing in his *Our Inheritance in the Great Pyramid*, "I have never accused, and do not propose to tax, those profane Egyptians with having had anything to do with the *design* of the Great pyramid," (33, p. 90). He called them, "Egyptian idolaters" with their "peculiar and alas! degrading religion," [sic] and their "vile hieratic system," (33, p. 6). He did not believe that the Egyptians built the Great Pyramid, proposing that it was designed by God Himself "'to be for a sign and for a witness unto the Lord of Hosts in the land of Egypt,'" (33, p. 596, quoting from Isaiah 19:20).

It is this type of blatant prejudice that has led modern archaeologists to hold all pyramidology as unworthy of consideration. In more than thirty years of studying ancient Egypt I have found there to be no interest among Egyptologists in even reviewing some of the less controversial elements of pyramidology and the timeline. On one occasion, one of the most famous of Egyptologists living today told me that there was absolutely no reason to consider such "pyramid–idiocy" since it was based in religious prejudice.

Despite all of this, the timeline in the Great Pyramid and the structure of the Great Pyramid show a remarkable correlation to world events, and this data can be obtained only from the pyramidologists. Let's attempt to review Davidson's diagram while overlooking his prejudicial statements and concepts.

We will also ignore Davidson's dash lines, finding them to be his conjectures in an effort to fit dates to Bible stories rather than actual passageways in the edifice or verses in the *Egyptian Book of the Dead*. Thus, his 4000 BC beginning for the Adamic race is his speculation, not supported by Egyptian texts or stones. We begin with the entrance to structure.

Use illustrations 20, 23, and 24 to follow along.

The Entrance:

In his diagram, Davidson marked the date for the entrance to the Great Pyramid at 2144 BC, and if one were standing at the entrance and imagined its descending passageway to be a telescope looking out to the stars, one would see that it points directly to the polar star. Our planet is not spinning fast enough to maintain a single pole star, thus its natural wobble, like a slow, spinning top, points to different circumpolar stars at different times. The Earth completes one wobble every 25,826.54 solar years, and if you drew a line from the North Pole into space, it would trace out a circle over the course of those 25,826.54 solar years. Walter Cruttenden, director of the Binary Research Institute, an archaeological–astronomical think tank in California, wrote: "Some people called it the *Yuga* cycle [Hindu], others called it the Grand cycle, and others the Perfect Year . . . But the most common name found in use from ancient Europe to ancient China, was simply the *Great Year.*" (11, pp. xix–xx.) The Great Year is often attributed to Plato's writings and astronomically to the Greek astronomer Hipparchus, who computed the true rate of one complete precession cycle at slightly less than 26,000 years. This cycle is also the time it takes our sun to pass through every constellation (sign) in the Zodiac, moving backward, so our age of Pisces moves into Aquarius, not Aries.

The major circumpolar stars for our planet are Thuban, Kochab, Polaris, Vega, Alrai, and Alderamin. Thuban was the closest star visible with the naked eye to the pole star from 3942 BC until about 1900 BC, when the much brighter Kochab began to approach the pole. Thuban was closest to the pole in 2787 BC, when it was less than two and a half arc–minutes away from the pole. However, as we learned earlier, astronomers have two dates for the pole to shine directly in view from the descending passageway of the Great Pyramid, 3350 BC and 2170 BC, with archaeologists stating that the 2170 BC is simply not the time of the building of the pyramid, leaving us with the 3350 BC date.

In addition to the Pole Star, Davidson also determined that the "arris edge" of the entrance aligned with the star Alcyone in the Pleiades Constellation (the "Seven Sisters"). The arris edge is an architectural term for the edge formed by the intersection of two surfaces at an angle. In this case, Davidson determined that *perpendicular* to the arris edges an imaginary line would be pointing to Alcyone in 2644 BC. Why Alcyone? In the myth of Alcyone, "Halcyon Days" are the seven days in winter when storms never occur, indicating *peaceful days*. This may indicate that the initiation time period or the deceased's transition time is seven days. But Halcyon Days also means to "harken back to an earlier time" and remember them as idyllic, so this may be the intention of the pyramid builders—remembering human origins are in the heavens, not the earth.

The Pleiades star cluster is one of the most ancient known objects in the heavens. Since they are only 4° off the zodiacal path in the sky, they are easily seen from Earth in the Northern and Southern hemispheres. The Seven Sisters are: Maia, Electra, Alcyone, Taygete, Asterope, Celaeno, and Merope. Only six of the seven primary stars are distinctly visible to the naked eye, but the ancients knew of the seventh star. The so-called "lost" star was explained in mythology as Merope deserting her sisters in shame, having taken a mortal husband, Sisyphus, the King of Corinth. Another explanation for the "lost" star is the myth of Electra who was an ancestress of the royal house of Troy. After the destruction of Troy, the grief stricken Electra abandoned her sisters and was transformed into a comet and became a sign of impending doom. In 2357 BC, Chinese astronomical texts contain reports of "The Blossom Stars," the ancient Chinese name for the Pleiades. In 1000 BC, Hesiod wrote poetically about these stars that were mythologically considered to be daughters of Atlas and Pleione the Oceanid. In his *The Astronomy* he wrote: "The Pleiades . . . whose stars are these—Lovely Teygata, and dark–faced Electra, and Alcyone, and bright Asterope, and Celaeno, and Maia, and Merope, whom glorious Atlas begot . . . In the mountains of Cyllene she (Maia, the eldest daughter of the seven Pleiades) bare Hermes, the herald of the gods." (15) And since Hermes is associated with Egyptian Thoth, this becomes significant to our study. In the 700s BC Homer spoke of the Pleiades in his *Odyssey* and *Iliad*. There are three direct references to the Pleiades in the Bible: in Job 9:9 and 38:31, and Amos 5:8, and an indirect reference in Revelation 1:16, which describes a vision of the coming of the Messiah holding seven stars in his right hand. North American Indian tribes have marvelous legends about the seven sisters, and in Hindu tradition Shiva created *Kartikeya* (also known as *Skanda*), whose name means: "him of the Pleiades." Obviously, the Pleiades were a significant cluster of stars to the ancient people. And since the ancient Egyptians believed that we all came from the stars and will return to them, it is not surprising that the Pleiades and Alcyone have an association with the entrance to the Great Pyramid.

Let's return to Davidson's diagram.

The entrance has some of the largest stones in the pyramid forming a corbeled *double* arch over the entrance. (See illustration 22.) Recall that in 24 BC Strabo wrote, "The Greater [pyramid], a little way up one side, has a stone that may be taken out, which being raised up [*sublato*, meaning to "take up," as in open upward], there is a sloping passage to the foundations [the descending passageway]." The unusual huge double arch and the hidden lifting door are a lot of unnecessary engineering and work unless they are intended to convey more than a simple entrance; which may be the case, for just below the double arch is the hieroglyph for the "horizon," indicating that this entrance is the "horizon of the Light" (*Ta Khut*, meaning "the Light," which was the Egyptian name for the Great Pyramid).

The Egyptian legend of the descent of the metaphysical godlings of the Creator out the realms of the stars and into the depths and density of matter is represented by the descending passageway leading from the entrance to the subterranean "Pit" in the bedrock beneath the Great Pyramid's structure (another amazing and seemingly unnecessary feature of design and construction unless it has meaning beyond a tomb). Davidson saw and wrote that the starlight shining down this descending passageway "symbolized the promise of ascent even whilst descent was taking place."

Using the guideline that the pyramid inch equals one year of time until reaching the Great Step when the pyramid inch equals one month, Davidson measured the passageways throughout the Great Pyramid, correlating his findings with the Bible stories. As we can see, he considered the date for the Exodus of Israelites out of Egypt and onto the Promised Land to correspond with the first ascending passageway.

In the *Egyptian Book of the Dead* there are many gates that must be passed. Davidson associates the entrance to the first ascending passageway with the Gate of the Ascent.

As we have learned, Davidson translated "The Hall of Double Ma'at" (also spelled Maat, goddess of truth) as "the double halls of truth." The first hall is the first ascending passageway, which Davidson called "Hall of Truth in Darkness," and considered to be Israel under the Yoke of the Law of Moses and the long journey through the desert to the Promised Land. The passageway is so low that an initiate would have to bend over possibly even duck–walk in order progress through this small but long passageway. As we can see in the diagram, Davidson's measurements reveal that the last step in the Hall of Truth in Darkness is dated to 4 BC, which he concluded must be the correct date for the birth of the Messiah Jesus. Davidson couldn't have known that roughly a century later researchers would uncover the edict issued by King Herod to kill all male children two years of age and younger in an effort to kill the newborn Jesus, and that it was dated by scholars to 4 BC.

One's head clears the low passageway at the date of 30 1/4 AD, which

Davidson assumed was the actual date of the crucifixion. Davidson identified this point with the passion of the Messiah. Egypt's Messiah was Horus, immaculately born of Isis, who conceived the child messiah with the help of Thoth's stirring and awaking her godly, limitless, life-giving powers. She and Horus suffered many trials brought on by the Egyptian Satan: Set. Set and the grown Horus eventually become the two combatants in the battle of the dark and the light in the *Egyptian Book of the Dead*.

Here we arrive at the passageway to the Queen's Chamber, which Davidson titled "Chamber of Second Birth" or "New Birth" and associated with the resurrection of Jesus and his teaching to Nicodemus about the need to be born a second time: "'Truly, I say to you, unless one is born anew, he cannot see the kingdom of God.' Nicodemus said to him, 'How can a man be born when he is old? Can he enter a second time into his mother's womb and be born?' Jesus answered, 'Truly, I say to you, unless one is born of water and the Spirit, he cannot enter the kingdom of God. That which is born of the flesh is flesh, and that which is born of the Spirit is spirit. Do not marvel that I said to you, "You must be born anew." The wind blows where it wills, and you hear the sound of it, but you do not know from whence it comes or whither it goes; so it is with everyone who is born of the Spirit.'" (John 3:4–8 RSV)

The second ascending passageway is the Grand Galley, which Davidson called "Hall of Truth in Light." He wrote that the first hall is passed while one is still uncertain about Divine guidance and one's relationship to God—as indicated by the Israelites building a golden calf to represent their god, then later destroying the calf and accepting an unseen God and His Ten Commandments as a covenant between God and the people. The second hall is the hall of truth through which one passes while possessing some enlightenment about the Divinity and one's relationship to the unseen God.

The Grand Gallery is just that, *grand!* When one finally makes it out of the first low ascending passageway, having struggled to ascend it in a bent-over position, and then stands up fully to see the next passageway, its grandeur is awe inspiring, even though it is another rising passage 153.1 feet long. It has seven corbelled walls ascending 28 feet above floor; each slab of wall is outset from the other by three inches. One is standing on a floor that is 6.8 feet wide, with the walls sloping inward to a high narrow ceiling that is only 3.4 feet wide, adding to the wonder of the magnificent hall. High up at the end of this upward sloping Grand Gallery is the Great Step, which is three feet high. Then there is another low passageway into the "Chamber of the Triple Veil," which subsequently leads into the King's Chamber.

As we saw earlier, the pyramid inch was derived from the sacred cubit of 25 inches and the measurement under the boss mark. Throughout the pyramid this inch is equivalent to one year of time, and Davidson uses this data. However, once we reach the floor to the King's Chamber, one pyramid inch is equivalent to one month. Time is twelve times faster than it has been. And we see this in Davidson's diagram.

Many, many researchers and writers have assumed that the Chamber of the Triple Veil was a portcullis, which is a strong, heavy stone sliding up and down in vertical grooves; when lowered it blocks a gateway to a fortress or town, or in this case the King's Chamber. Portcullis comes from the French *porte coulissante*, meaning "gliding door." However, some of the researchers who took a closer look at this strange chamber have concluded that it was not a portcullis. The Edgar brothers are among these, writing: " . . . when, however, we begin to investigate the subject more closely . . . we find that there are distinctive peculiarities about the 'granite leaf' [this is the one with the boss mark], which make it certain that it, at all events, had not been intended by the architect to serve as a portcullis [a blocking stone]." (14, p. 488)

On the other hand, J.P. Lepre spent fifteen years in the 1970s and '80s investigating the pyramids of Egypt, focusing on the Great Pyramid, and he found the other four fractured granite stones and matched them to the grooves in the Chamber of the Triple Veil, giving much evidence that this was indeed a portcullis, that could block passage to the King's Chamber when the stones were lowered. He published his findings in his book, *The Egyptian Pyramids*. (See Bibliography for details.)

As to the timeline, each lower passage is a time of hardship in the world. In Davidson's diagram (See illustration 23.) the first low passage is the time of "the war to end all wars," World War I (1914–1918). Recall that in Fatima, Portugal, on October 13, 1917 Mary, the mother of Jesus, appeared to three children and prophesied the end of WWI but foretold that an even greater war was coming, World War II. But she also told the children to pray hard for the souls and church in Russia because within days atheism would take control. Bolshevik–Soviet Revolution began with the takeover of government buildings on October 24, 1917, known as "Red October," and atheistic communism took over Russia. In 1922 the *Bezbozhnik* magazine (literally, "The Godless" magazine) was publishing antireligious articles. State atheism in the Soviet Union was known as *gosateizm* and was based on the ideology of Marxism-Leninism. Lenin was the founder of the Soviet state and wrote the infamous line: "Religion is the opium of the people." The new Soviet state expropriated all church property, including the churches themselves, and in the period from 1922 to 1926, twenty–eight Russian Orthodox bishops and more than 1,200 priests were killed, and a much greater number was subjected to persecution. When we consider how much of the ancient Egyptian attention was devoted to spirituality, especially as related to the *Egyptian Book of the Dead* and the Great Pyramid, it is more likely that this low passage (always an indication of hardship and effort) relates more to the spiritual loss than the socio–economic one.

Once through the Chamber of the Triple we must bend again for another low and longer passageway. The second low passage begins with the early stages of the Great Depression (1929–1939) and its devastating effects in virtually every country on the planet and every socio-economic stratum from rich to poor. The Great Depression ended with the start of World War II (1939–1945), and the war ended in the middle of the King's Chamber or the Chamber of the Open Tomb (1945).

Interestingly, in this Chamber of the Open Tomb, Lepre discovered a stone in the west wall of the Chamber that does not fit the positioning of all the others in this room, and he surmised that this could indeed be a removable stone revealing another passageway or chamber. To this date, no one has attempted to move the stone and investigate.

Davidson's timeline ends when it reaches the south wall of the Chamber in 1953. Davidson was sure the End Times were upon us and the "Judgment of All Nations" (as he called it) would begin. However, from another source that we will study more about shortly, we learn that Davidson was supposed to go up the wall to the apex above the Chamber of the Open Tomb. (See illustration 24.)

As we can now see, the pyramid timeline continues through the five granite layers to the mitered limestone blocks forming the vaulted ceiling at the top of the chamber's complete structure. Thus, the prophetic timeline actually ends in 2038.

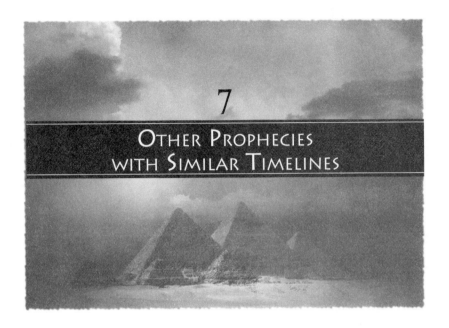

7

OTHER PROPHECIES WITH SIMILAR TIMELINES

(Prophesied Line of the Popes Ends Soon—2038?)

Perhaps one of the best measurements of the progression of prophecies for our times is the succession of the Popes. Three different prophets gave clear and measurable information about the predicted line of the Popes: Bishop Malachy, the Monk of Padua, and Nostradamus. Furthermore, apparitions of Mary, the mother of Jesus, gave information about papal succession in her apparitions in Fatima and Garabandal. Let's explore this information.

In 1138, an Irish bishop named Malachy visited the Vatican. While there, he fell into a deep trance during which he saw the reigning pontiff and the line of succession of 112 Popes, followed by the final fall of the Church of Rome as we have known it. When he awoke, he wrote a complete manuscript on the vision, giving each Pope a Latin motto. The manuscript was sent to the Vatican after Malachy's passing, where it

71

was stored in secret archives until 1590, long after Nostradamus' death (1503–1566). Later, around 1730–40, a monk called "The Monk of Padua" wrote a manuscript listing a sequence of Popes and the ultimate end of the papacy that closely followed Malachy's, also using Malachy's mottos for the Popes.)

Of the twentieth century Popes, Malachy gave Benedict XV the motto *Religio Depopulata*, which could relate to his being the Pope during WWI, certainly a period of "depopulation of religion." Pius XII, 1939 to 1958, Malachy called *Pastor Angelicus*, referring to his angelic shepherding of the Church, which many inside and outside of the church acknowledged. Many followers considered this Pope to be among the most saintly. He was followed by John XXIII, 1958–63, whom Malachy called *Pastor et Nauta* ("Shepherd and Navigator"), perhaps referring to his position as Archbishop of Venice. This pope also reconvened the Ecumenical Council for the first time since 1869, and the Council used the symbols of a cross and a ship, perhaps indicative of the Shepherd and Navigator. After John XXIII came *Flos Florum* ("Flower of Flowers") for Paul VI (1963–78). His coat of arms contained a floral design. After Paul VI came *De Mediatate Lunae* ("the middle or half of the moon"). This was John Paul I (August 26 to September 28, 1978). This is one of the shortest and most suspicious papal reigns in history. John Paul I was only sixty-six and in good health when he suddenly died. He had disturbed his Curia (Senate of Cardinals) by stating in one of his earliest speeches that God was not only the Heavenly Father but also the Heavenly Mother. He began to openly support women's rights and agreed to meet with a U.S. Congressional delegation to discuss artificial birth control! On the eve of his curious death, he asked his Secretary of State, Cardinal Jean Villot, to begin an investigation of the Vatican Bank because of his concern that Mafia money was being laundered through the bank. He also asked him to begin an investigation into secret memberships of his priests in the Freemason's Lodge. The next morning he was dead. Italian police investigators were surprised that Cardinal Villot initially gave them false information during their questioning and that the cardinals quickly embalmed the pope's body and then cremated it, against strict Catholic custom at that time. Stranger still, Cardinal Villot died within six months of these events. Here's what Nostradamus wrote four hundred years prior to this:

> *When the sepulchre of the great Roman is found*
> *The day after will be elected a Pope*
> *By his Senate he will not be approved*
> *Poisoned is his blood by the sacred chalice.* 3:65
>
> And,
>
> *He who will have government of the Great Cape [the Pope]*
> *Will be led to take action*
> *The twelve Red Ones [Cardinals] will come to spoil the cover*
> *Under murder, murder will come to be done.* 4:11

The passage "under murder, murder will come to be done," may refer to the poisoning (a murder), then the cremation (another murder for at that time Vatican law forbid it). If this death is ever found to be murder, the scandal would rock the papacy to its foundations, perhaps changing it forever.

If murder and Mafia connections aren't enough to shake the Vatican, pedophilia by priests who cannot maintain their vows of celibacy may be the scandal that brings on the end of the Roman Catholic Church. These types of scandals in all religions and denominations are being seen more and more. We've seen leaders of massive congregations go down in flaming scandals of moral and financial corruption. Perhaps there will come a day when the sacred will be desolate of true spiritual and moral light.

In Malachy's papal lineage, after John Paul I, comes *De Labore Solis* ("the labor of the sun"). The following pope was John Paul II, Karol Wojtyla from Poland. J.H. Brennan, author of some of the best books on Nostradamus, points out that the part of Poland from which John Paul II came was originally a portion of ancient France, and therefore the following quatrain may refer to him:

> *Not from Spain, but from ancient France*
> *He will be elected from the trembling ship*
> *To the enemy he will make assurance*
> *Who in his reign will be a cruel blight.* 5:49

Brennan considers the trembling ship to be the Church itself. The great enemy of Polish John Paul II would have been none other than the Soviet Union. John Paul II made assurances (line 3) to the Soviets concerning the strikes in Poland by the workers, assurances that may have kept the Soviets from invading as they did in Hungary and Czechoslovakia. It is said that John Paul II sent a message to Moscow that if they mounted an invasion against Poland, he would fly to Warsaw and stand in full papal regalia before the approaching tanks. Brennan goes on to say that though John Paul II was successful in this situation, the Soviet blight (line 4) continued through much of his early years as Pope. Then there came the first assassination attempt by Mehmet Ali Agca, a Turk who shot John Paul II. It was believed that the Soviet KGB was behind the shooting.

The second assassination attempt, which received little press, caught more of Nostradamus' attention:

> *Oh great Rome, your ruin comes close*
> *Not of your walls, but of your blood and substance*
> *The sharp one of letters will be so horrible a notch*
> *Pointed steel placed up his sleeve, ready to wound.* 10:65

The second assassin attempt came during a papal visit to Portugal in 1982 by an educated priest who pulled a long knife from out of his sleeve and attempted to kill John Paul II. This quatrain seems to clearly express Nostradamus' vision of this event, noting even its failure, "your ruin comes *close*."

After John Paul II, Malachy and the Priest of Padua predict only two more popes: *Gloria Olivae* ("glory of the olive") and *Petrus Romanus* ("Peter of Rome"). Malachy predicts that Peter of Rome will be the last Pope, and that the city will be burned. The Monk of Padua also predicts the burning of the city when the last Pope sits on the throne. Nostradamus wrote:

> *The great star for seven days will burn*
> *A cloud will make two suns appear*
> *The big mastiff will howl all night*
> *When a great Pope changes his territory.* 2:41

If the Vatican is burned, then the Pope would have to change his territory, at least temporarily. Since the olive is a Jewish icon, many people believed that the Archbishop of Paris, Cardinal Jean-Marie Lustiger, born a Jew and converted to Catholicism, would be the next pope. But when the German Cardinal Joseph Ratzinger was chosen, most everyone considered Malachy's prophecy to have failed. But when Cardinal Ratzinger took the name "Benedict XVI," he consciously or unconsciously fulfilled the prophecy of Malachy. How? The Benedictine order is also known as the "Olivetans," after the Mt. of Olives, and the leader of the Olivetans would be the "Glory of the Olive"!

Malachy's last pope is *Petrus Romanus*, "Peter of Rome." Is St. Peter—considered to have been the first pope—to be the last pope? There is some precedence for this in that Elijah was to return as the forerunner of the Messiah, and in the Matthew 17:10-13 we find even Jesus supporting this idea: "The disciples asked him [Jesus], 'Then why do the scribes say that first Elijah must come?' He replied, 'Elijah does come, and he is to restore all things; but I tell you that Elijah has already come, and they did not know him, but did to him whatever they pleased. So also the Son of man will suffer at their hands.' Then the disciples understood that he was speaking to them of John the Baptist."

It will be interesting to see how the timing of Malachy's vision fits the Pyramid timeline of 2038.

Marian Prophecies

In the many Marian apparitions (visions of Mary, the mother of Jesus), the Popes and their successions were foretold. During her apparition in Fatima, Portugal in 1917, she said the "war that was to end all wars" (WWI) would be followed by an even worse war (WWII). She also said the second war would occur during the reign of a Pope named "Pius XI" (specifically named by Mary in 1917 but he did not become pope until 1936).

In her apparition in Garabandal, Spain in the 1960s, one of the little girls who saw and heard the apparition, Conchita, said that the Blessed Mother told her that there would be only two more Popes after Paul VI. Here are Conchita's own words on this: "The Blessed Virgin said in 1962 that there will be only two more Popes after Paul VI. But this does not mean that the world will come to an end." Now we know the papal prophecies of Malachy, the Monk of Padua, and Nostradamus' don't agree with this. The Popes during the Garabandal apparitions were John XXIII (1958–63) and then Paul VI (1963–78). Following Conchita's statement, the next pope, John Paul II, would then be the last pope. John Paul II came out and stated that the two failed assassinations changed the destiny of the papal line, allowing for two more popes.

Mayan-Aztec Prophecy

Let's begin by understanding why the ancient Mayan stargazers pointed to 2012 as a major milestone in the evolution of humankind. The Mesoamerican prophecy identifies 2012 as the end of an age that they called the "Sun of Movement." "Sun" in this context means a Sun cycle, so we can consider this to be an "age," thus the "Age of Movement" or "Age of Change." Inscriptions on Mayan stelae (tall sculpted stone slabs or columns) indicate that this age began on August 13, 3114 BC (4 Ahau 8 Cumku). It officially ends on this Winter Solstice, December 21, 2012 (4 Ahau 3 Kankin). These two dates are regarded as the beginning-date and end-date of a 5,125-year-long cycle in the Mayan Long Count Calendar, a course of thirteen measurements of time called "bak'tuns." In addition to this calendar, the Mayans foresaw a rare galactic alignment of our star, the Sun.

They determined that the Sun would be positioned directly between Earth and the very center of the Milky Way Galaxy on the Winter Solstice of 2012. This celestial event is rare, occurring only every 25,826.54 years. This is the time it takes the Sun to pass through all twelve of the signs of the zodiac, which are actually star constellations: Aries, Taurus, and so on; but the Sun moves through them backwards; so, Pisces, Aquarius, and so on. This is why we are moving out of the Age of Pisces into the Aquarian Age.

It takes the Sun hundreds of years to completely cross the cluster of stars in the Milky Way, but the Sun is aligning with the very center portion of the Milky Way in these times that we are living in. It began entering the central region in the year 1998. In the next chapter we'll see that the reincarnated high priest from ancient Egypt also pointed to 1998 as a beginning of the change from one age to another. Here is that prediction:

> "In 1998 we may find a great deal of the activities as have been wrought by the gradual changes that are coming about. These are at the periods when the cycle of the solar activity, or the years as related to the sun's passage through the various spheres of activity become paramount to the change between the Piscean and the Aquarian age. This is a *gradual*, not a cataclysmic activity in the experience of the earth in this period." 1602-3

A key to what the Mayans believed will happen in 2012 is found on a monument at El Tortuguero (literally, "the turtle catcher") in Tabasco, Mexico. Though the aged stone message is missing some glyphs, many trained interpreters have agreed that the message goes something like this:

> "Long ago it happened, on the day of the Sacred Beginning when the Becoming-Ripe-House was completed. It was the Underworld house of Ahkal K'uk [more on terms and names in a moment]. It is many years when the Thirteenth Bak'tun will end on December 21, 2012. Then it will happen, darkness, and Bolon Yokte' K'uh will descend to the . . . [here the glyph is completely missing from the stone]."

To understand the terms and names used in this passage, we have to approach as if it were a dream, like Dreamtime in Aboriginal legends, and with more details on the Mayan cosmology. For example, the Becoming-Ripe-House is very likely the prototype physical body for the Children of God to use when pressing themselves into matter in those early times of first incarnations during the "Sacred Beginning." This is what the reincarnated high priest referred to when he spoke of the beginning and quoted a passage from the biblical book of Job: "We find the entity was among those in the day when the forces of the Universe came together, when there was upon the waters the sound of the coming together of the Sons of God, when 'the morning stars sang together,' and over the face of the waters there was the voice of the glory of the coming of the plane for man's dwelling." (341-1)

In order to understand the two names in the Mayan message we have to first understand that in Mayan cosmology the original gods were comparable to cosmic forces or states of consciousness and activity rather than to beings. Over time these original gods became individualized, even incarnate, but their original influence was as a force or condition or state of consciousness. And they may return or descend or arise again to influence life on Earth. This is the case with Ahkal K'uk and Bolon Yokte' K'uh. (We may also consider the Underworld to be a realm or state of consciousness, comparable to the subconscious mind—a subconscious of both individual minds and the collective mind. From these levels many powerful unseen forces influence life (individually and collectively), often surprising the physical world and outer consciousness, and even challenging the heavenly thoughts and influences.)

Both Ahkal and Bolon Yokte' have a connection to the original creation (the title K'uk or K'uh simply means "god" or "lord"). Ahkal is associated with a most powerful creation god named Itzamna, who created "First Father" and "Lady Beastie," the parents of beautiful Palenque's Triad gods—strangely named GI, GII, and GIII. Ahkal may be correlated with the godly portion inside every soul, which is inside the physical body, which is the Becoming-Ripe-House of Ahkal. Bolon Yokte' is a plural name commonly translated as Nine Steps or Nine Paths. Nine Paths is a god of the Underworld, thus the subconscious mind. Nine Paths is also the energy and spirit of the warrior or contender, as was biblical Jacob who wrestled with God and received the name Israel, meaning "he who contends with God." (See Genesis 32:24–30.) Of course, he contends with God in order to be blessed and know God better.

With all of this in mind, we may translate this Mayan message to mean: "An event that has occurred before will occur again, thus a cycle comes around again, ending one period and beginning another. The original event is associated with the sacred beginning of life incarnate in this world and a physical house—a body—that may become a temple for the living God (the little "I am" of the Great I AM). This body was and is the unseen house of each soul's godly, eternal, and immortal nature, made in the image of God (Genesis 1:26). Many years have led up to the end of this age of movement or change, and when it ends this world and its limited awareness will appear dark, and then the contender returns from our deeper mind and will destroy the illusion."

One degree of our Sun's movement is 72 years, so dating a major change to the year 2012 and another to the year 2038 is virtually placing them within the same time. Among some of the Mayan Elders, the year 2012 is seen as the *beginning of* a transitional period that they believe will be in full movement by the year 2038—and at the time one of them shared this information, he and his colleagues had no knowledge of the Great Pyramid's timeline date also being 2038.

8

AN EGYPTIAN HIGH PRIEST REINCARNATES

I realize how odd this title appears to some Western readers, but much of the Eastern half of the world accepts reincarnation as a natural cycle in a soul's eternal, immortal journey. Surprisingly, there has been good scientific research into reincarnation to give much credence to it. Consider the research of psychiatrist, biochemist, and university professor Ian Stevenson, MD (1918–2007).

While the head of the Department of Psychiatry at the University of Virginia (1957–2002), Dr. Stevenson conducted years of research into children who had past-life memories in which the past incarnation could be verified. He published his findings in 1966 in his attention-getting book *Twenty Cases Suggestive of Reincarnation*. A second and enlarged edition was published in 1974. Then in 1997 he published *Reincarnation and Biology: A Contribution to the Etiology of Birthmarks and Birth Defects Volume 1: Birthmarks*, followed that same year by *Reincarnation and Biology: A Contribution to the Etiology of Birthmarks and Birth Defects Volume 2: Birth Defects and*

Other Anomalies. In these two volumes he gave photographic evidence that past-life experiences carry over into this present life, even into the physical body's cellular memory, which manifests through birthmarks, defects, and irregularities.

To research his hypothesis, Dr. Stevenson set up a network of volunteers to find small children between two and four years of age who spontaneously began to talk about parents or siblings of a life he or she led in another time and place. He then carefully questioned both the family of the living child and the family of the deceased to ensure that they had no contact and that no information had been passed between them. He would obtain detailed information about the deceased, including information not fully known to anyone involved, such as details of the will, then he would use this information to verify that the child actually did know the details required. If some verification of the child's recall was realized, then the members of the two families would visit each other and ask the child whether he recognized places, objects, and people of his supposed previous existence.

Dr. Stevenson concluded that reincarnation was the "best possible explanation" for the following reasons:

1. The large number of witnesses and the lack of apparent motivation and opportunity, due to the vetting process, make the hypothesis of fraud extremely unlikely.
2. The large amount of information possessed by the child is not generally consistent with the hypothesis that the child obtained that information through investigated contact between the families.
3. Demonstration of similar personality characteristics and skills not learned in the current life and the lack of motivation for the long length of identification with a past life make the hypothesis of the child gaining his recollections and behavior through extra-sensory perception improbable.
4. When there is correlation between congenital deformities or birthmarks possessed by the child and the history of the previous individual, the hypothesis of random occurrence is improbable.

Fascinatingly, when Dr. Stevenson revisited the children in their teens, most could no longer remember their past-life; some could not even remember telling him about a past life. It was as though their minds were no longer in touch with those verified memories and they were now completely immersed in this incarnation.

Reincarnation is not the return of the personality of a previous lifetime, but the return of the deeper soul self and soul mind. The purpose of reincarnation is to help the soul grow to its ultimate potential as a conscious, living being in and beyond this world of materiality and three dimensions.

Before we review the story of the reincarnation of the high priest in ancient Egypt, we need to consider the nature and value of psychic information, because much of the high priest's story comes from psychically received knowledge.

The term "psychic" comes from the Greek word *psychikos*, meaning "of the mind, mental." A person who receives psychic information is using extra sensory perception—in other words, perception beyond the five normal senses of the body-mind, which are: seeing, tasting, smelling, hearing, and touching. *Psychikos* is derived from the Greek word *psyche*, which literally means "breath," and is associated with the life force inside each person, akin to "spirit." It has also been used to mean "soul," as in Aristotle's theory of the "three souls" ("three psyches") in *Peri Psûchês*.

But, like pyramidology, psychic information has become muddled in all sorts of occult phenomena and questionable or even phony psychic activity and information. Nevertheless, there are psychics and collections of psychic information that have been substantiated and are accepted as valuable knowledge from an extraordinary source.

One of the most famous and well-documented psychics is Edgar Cayce (1877-1945) and his over 14,000 psychic discourses maintained at his continuing center in Virginia Beach, Virginia, USA. The Edgar Cayce Foundation and the Association for Research and Enlightenment (A.R.E.) maintain 14,306 "readings" by the late Edgar Cayce. 581 of these discourses contain information about ancient Egypt. Among these readings on Egypt, 219 contain information identifying Edgar Cayce as the reincarnation of an Egyptian High Priest known as Ra-Ta. This Ra-Ta was involved with others in the conception, design, and building of the Great Pyramid. Of interest to us is that in 1932, long after many of the classical works of pyramidology had been published, Cayce was asked to psychically review the deductions and conclusions published in David Davidson and H. Aldersmith's *The Great Pyramid: Its Divine Message*. From his psychic state, he replied: "They are correct, though in some, far overdrawn." This is so typical of pyramidology, its fundament information is correct, especially measurements and correlations with the *Egyptian Book of the Dead*, but then it often goes beyond reasonable associations and conclusions, or is "overdrawn," as Cayce noted.

An example of Cayce's correlation of the passageways in the Great Pyramid to events in the human journey is the Great Depression that began in 1929. As we have seen, David Davidson and H. Aldersmith also saw the Great Depression in the Great Pyramid timeline. It began at the low passageway just after the antechamber to the King's Chamber, or the Chamber of the Open Tomb. (See illustration 24.)

In 1932 Cayce was asked about the end of the Great Depression; he replied that the financial hardships were not over but that the minds of human beings were changing to a better state that would allow improvements to come. However, Cayce stated that these difficult financial times would end between 1950 and 1958—this period marked a post WWII economic boom in the U.S., with an increase in manufacturing and home construction (Cayce gave this prophecy in 1932). Now most researchers would say that the Great Depression ended when the military mobilization in the U.S. reached it economic power stroke in 1941 starting one of the greatest booms in the history of this country, but it appears that Cayce didn't see true relief coming until *after* World War II and into the 1950s.

Despite his comments about the Great Depression and the Great Pyramid, Cayce considered the pyramid timeline to be more about religious and spiritual activity rather than political and economic events.

Cayce stated that the passageways through the Great Pyramid are constructed to express periods through which the world has passed and is passing in relation to religious and spiritual experiences of humanity. When low passages are reached, it indicates a downward trend. When expansive openings are reached, it is a buoyant, upward trend in human thought and action. This is also true of the variations in the color, character, and type of stone, as well as in the various turns in direction throughout the ancient edifice. He said that all changes which came in the religious thought in the world are shown in variations of the stone and passageways through the Great Pyramid and inside the King's Chamber from the open tomb to the top of the so-called relieving chambers, where the limestones meet in a vaulted ceiling above the five layers of granite stone ceilings.

Changes are also indicated numerically and astronomically. He said that accurate imaginary lines may be drawn from the original opening of the pyramid to the Pole Star Polaris. We see this on the north side of the Step Pyramid at Saqqara where the little hut has two holes drilled in stone for eyes to view the Pole Star. According to Cayce, this indicates that it is the stellar system toward which souls take flight after having completed their sojourn on planet Earth. He explained that gradual changes in the position of Polaris and the Dipper and the opening to the pyramid indicate changes in the human race. Souls from legendary Atlantis, Lemuria, La, Ur, Da, and other ancient civilizations will begin reincarnating in greater numbers. He said they would bring with them their innate knowledge of unseen forces, resulting in amazing advances in technology, communication, and creature comforts.

When asked when construction of the Great Pyramid began and how long it took to finish, he answered with dates that stretch credulity. But his answer is complex because in one of his readings he indicated that the activities of the pyramid builders had been begun by the ancient people using what we would call today "archaeology" to locate and uncover ancient mounds in Egypt, which were considered to be sacred places on the planet's surface—even rare portals that led out of earthly dimensions to realms beyond the planet. The Egyptians believed that there were "passageways" or portals to other realms. Then, when these mounds were found and sufficiently excavated, they built their new monuments on top of them, just as the ancient peoples in Mesoamerica. Cayce indicates that the Egyptians also added to their monuments from time to time. Of course our archaeological research today supports this activity. A good example would be the Karnak Temple in which each regime felt the need to add its piece to the mammoth complex.

The actual date that the Cayce's readings gave for the beginning of construction on the Great Pyramid was 10,490 BC! Cayce's readings state that the Great Pyramid was completed in 10,390 BC, requiring 100 years to construct. Despite how strange these dates are, the recent observation that the Sphinx Pit was eroded by tropical rainwater runoff rather than wind has pushed the dating of that monument back to 9000 BC or older. And the aforementioned discovery in a large basin region known as Nabta Playa, located about 62 miles west of Abu Simbel near the Egyptian–Sudanese border, with a Stonehenge–like calendar circle of stones dated to 4500 BC but belonging to a culture that may date back as far as 11,000 BC. This Nabta Playa Stonehenge reveals advanced skill in building and celestial mapping, making it possible that such skills existed in much more ancient times than originally thought. These may actually be the originators, or at least carriers, of the *Egyptian Book of the Dead* content and remnants of David Davidson's pre–Egypt sophisticated culture who brought the sacred cubit to Egypt.

When asked how the Great Pyramid was built, Cayce answered cryptically, "By the use of those forces in nature as make for iron to swim. Stone floats in the air in the same manner. This will be discovered in '58." (5748-6) Of course Archimedes (ca 287 to 212 BC), who studied in Alexandria, Egypt with Euclid, explained how iron floats on water: Water's destiny is such that any object sitting on it experiences an upward force equal to the weight of the water displaced by the object. The average density of a boat—the combination of the iron and the air—is very light compared to the average density of water. So very little of the boat actually has to submerge into the water before the water has displaced the weight of the boat. Another factor for large ships is the buoyancy of air-tight compartments.

Given these details about iron floating on water, how would stone float in the air? We might assume that Cayce is referring to hot–air balloons or lighter–than–air gas balloons, possibly moored or tethered next to the construction site. However, it is hard to imagine how such balloons could lift the weight of the stones in the Great Pyramid.

Another possibility is a kite–like device that could lift or drag very heavy stones in a modest wind. In January 2004, Maureen Clemmons, a presenter at the Cayce Center, and Caltech aeronautics expert Mory Gharib raised a nearly four ton, 15-foot–high obelisk using only a kite, a pulley system, and a support frame. The wind was not steady, which is the ideal, but was gusting up to 22 miles an hour. When a gust came, they raised the obelisk in 25 seconds—so quickly that the concrete-and-rebar obelisk was lifted off the ground completely and swung free for a few seconds. Once the motion steadied, the obelisk was lowered to an upright position. The average weight of the pyramid stones is 2.5 tons, which means that relatively small kites could have been used to move and lift these stones, and very quickly too.

Keep in mind that bones of the numerous men needed to build the pyramid have not been found. Whether with slave labor or as has been recently suggested, with the nationwide labor of inspired citizen–volunteers, there would have to much more evidence of their presence than has been found—and that includes Lehner's workers camps. In 1586 the Vatican moved a 330–ton Egyptian obelisk to St. Peter's Square; lifting the stone required 74 horses and 900 men using ropes and pulleys. The Great Pyramid has roughly 2,300,000 stones in it. Where are the bones of the labor force needed to construct such an edifice? Also, the remains of the giant ramps around the pyramid, which archaeologists theorize were used to raise the stones, have not been found either. In fact, there are no archaeological traces of how this pyramid was constructed. (Clemmons' and Gharib's kite method would not have left any traces and would have been easy to clean up once the work was completed.)

According to Cayce's psychic readings, there are three record chambers located in three separate locations on the planet. Each has an identical set of stone records. One set is under the waters near the Bahamian island of Bimini near the Gulf Stream in a sunken Atlantean temple. The second set is beneath an overhanging temple in the Mayan lands. The third set is underground near the Sphinx in Giza, Egypt. According to Cayce's readings, each of the record halls will be found and opened. Each cache contains the same story on thirty-two stone tablets—they are three sets of the same story.

Cayce explained that the set in the waters of the Bahamas is in a submerged temple beneath the slime of ages belonging to an Atlantean high priest and governor named Atlan, who mistakenly believed that he could safely keep a set of the tables in this region of Atlantis, even though the continent was going through serious physical changes resulting from earthquakes, heightened volcanic activity, and even the "fiery rain" of terrible meteor showers. These fiery meteors showers created the Carolina Bays and the Puerto Rican Trench. Atlan underestimated the destructive power of the earth changes, and his temple along with this portion of Atlantis sank beneath the sea. Cayce said that this temple "will rise and is rising again." (2012-1)

The set of records hidden in the Mayan lands belonged to another Atlantean a high priest named Iltar, who sailed from sinking Atlantis and first stored his tablets in a temple he built in the Yucatan Peninsula. However, Iltar's first temple was destroyed when another inundation occurred in nearby portions of Atlantis. Iltar was forced to take his stone tablets and move deeper into the Mayan lands. Cayce's readings indicate that he then stored them at the massive Mayan site at Piedras Negras, Guatemala, called Y-Okib by the Mayans, meaning the "entrance" or "cave," located just over the border of Mexico in Guatemala. Iltar likely entered the Usumacinta River and travel to the Piedras Negras site, which is on a high hill at a bend in the river. Cayce said that Iltar's temple will "rise again." In our times archaeologists have conducted many explorations of the massive Mayan temple complex at Piedras Negras, but it is a very difficult place to explore.

The records stored in Egypt are in a subterranean chamber off the right front paw of the Sphinx in line with the Great Pyramid. In another discourse he clearly stated that the Egyptian record cache is between the Nile and the Sphinx. (The old Nile, before the dam, came right up to the Giza Plateau. Archaeologists have found the harbor in front of the Valley Temple next to the Sphinx.)

(Cayce's readings also said that the base of the sphinx was "laid out in channels," and in the left rear corner of the Sphinx, which is facing the Great Pyramid, one can find the wording of how the Sphinx was "founded, giving the history of the first invading ruler, Arart," of the tribe that invaded from Mt. Ararat.

The Hall of Records in Yucatan may also be laid out in underground channels because both Mayan and Aztec complexes are known to have underground tunnels, chambers, and passage ways.

Cayce stated, "as time draws nigh when changes are to come about, there may be the opening of those three places where the records are one, to those that are the initiates in the knowledge of the One God . . ." (5750-1)

According to Cayce, the three record caches contain stone tablets, linens, gold, and artifacts of import to the cultures that stored them. He indicated that mummified bodies are also buried with the records. As to the question about what language the records may be in, Cayce did not answer directly, saying only that this was a time when the entire world spoke one language, a time prior to the Tower of Babel legend in the Bible. Therefore, we could assume that each set of the records is in the same language as the others. In one reading he indicated that the Atlanteans had a slightly different dialect or perhaps pronunciation of the worldwide language than the rest of the world. In another reading (2329-3), he actually stated that there are exactly "thirty-two tablets or plates" in the Egyptian hall of records. He said that these tablets would require interpretation, and this interpretation would take some time. Let's hope it does not take as long as the interpretation of the Dead Sea Scrolls of the Qumran caves.

The records are from Atlantis. They recount the times of the beginning when "the Spirit took form" and began to enter bodies. They recount the development of these bodies and these people throughout the ancient era of legendary Lemuria and Atlantis and the new peoples' subsequent migrations to new lands, including early Egypt. The records also describe the final destruction of Atlantis and the new construction in Egypt. Cayce said they contain the *who, what, where,* and *when* of these ancient times and the rediscovery that is to come in our times. (378-16)

With his eyes closed and breathing rhythmically while his longtime stenographer Gladys Davis quietly recorded the spoken words in shorthand, Cayce explained how the ancient ones were actually "rebuilding" already aged monuments on the "plains" of Giza as well as building new ones. Among the rebuilding projects was the Sphinx, which is, according to Cayce, older than the Great Pyramid. He directed our attention to the buildings that connect to the Sphinx—the Sphinx Temple and the Valley Temple.

He described how a Temple of Isis was lost during the ancient deluge "centuries before" the Sphinx existed. Cayce dates this great flood to 22,006 BC, so his dates are long before any archaeologist's dates for early Egypt. Cayce's predynastic period begins with builders who were invaders of Egypt, coming from the area of Mt. Ararat—connecting them to the supposed resting place of Noah's ark. These invaders were the demigods of ancient Egyptian lore and carved the amazing Sphinx (ca 10,700 BC) prior to the building of the Great Pyramid (195-14), which occurred between 10,490 and 10,390 BC. (5748-6) Many archaeologists have found and published evidence of a significant influence in Egypt from peoples along the Euphrates and Tigris Rivers, Lake Van, and Mt. Ararat.

Around this time a surviving band of Atlanteans arrived on the Egyptian shores with their precious prehistoric tablets in tow. The Egyptians and Atlanteans agreed to build what Cayce called variously a "pyramid of records" (239-7), a "hall of records" (519-1), and a "tomb of records" (2329-2) in front of the Sphinx.

When asked where this record cache exactly was, Cayce said it was between the Sphinx and the Nile. (378-16 and 5748-5) He also said that the "storehouse" was "facing the Sphinx" (5748-5) and in "a pyramid of its own." (2329-3)

Cayce said that there were underground "connecting chambers from the Sphinx's right paw" to the records. (378-16) (The Dream Stela of Tuthmosis IV that sits between the front legs of the Sphinx reveals an underground chamber with a door.) Ground-penetrating radar conducted in the 1990s revealed an anomaly beneath the Sphinx that may well be this chamber. I have been all over this sight more than thirty times and can assure you that we are going to need the miraculous, magical help of the Spirit to find these records. As Cayce said, it cannot be entered until "the time has been fulfilled," and it "may not be entered without an understanding, for those that were left as guards may not be passed until after a period of their regeneration in the Mount, or the fifth root race begins." (5748-6) The fifth root race is an evolving people with new, enlightened bodies that are coming during the shift to the new era. The regeneration in the Mount refers to our crown chakras being regenerated. Cayce's insights into these most mystical concepts are very ethereal and otherworldly. He sees the climax of evolution as the return to our spirit-nature from whence we originally descended into matter.

When people would ask Edgar Cayce if they could be a part of the discovery and interpretation of these records, he would answer yes, but

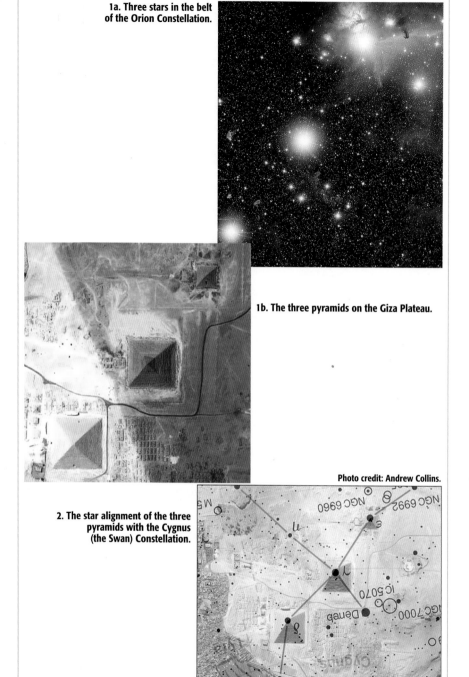

1a. Three stars in the belt of the Orion Constellation.

1b. The three pyramids on the Giza Plateau.

Photo credit: Andrew Collins.

2. The star alignment of the three pyramids with the Cygnus (the Swan) Constellation.

3a. Photo of the eight sloping sides of the Great Pyramid by British Air Force Brigadier-General P. R. C. Groves, 1940.

3b. Ikonos satellite image of the eight sides of the Great Pyramid.

4. The few remaining limestone casing stones on the Great Pyramid.

5. The so-called "Boss Mark" that was used as a measuring device. It is located in the Chamber of the Triple Veil. This is the view looking up into the first chamber.

6. Text of the Book of the Dead on the walls of the Unas Pyramid.

Photo Credit: Smithsonian Museum.

7. The "Egyptian Stonehenge" at Nabta Playa.

Photo Credit: Raymbetz, Groupe d'Études Égypte

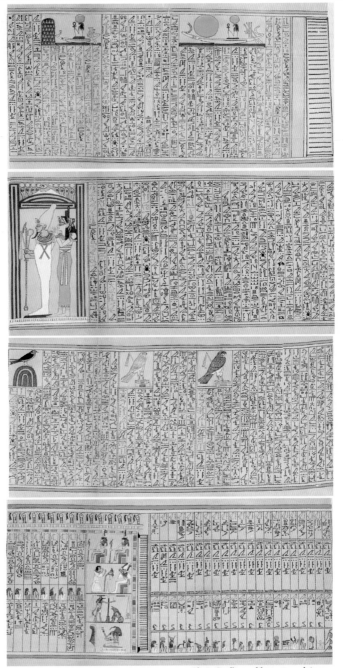

8. Portions of the "Papyrus of Ani" (ca 1250 BC, Nineteenth Dynasty) from Wallis Budge's *The Book of the Dead*, published by Longman & Co. in London in 1899.

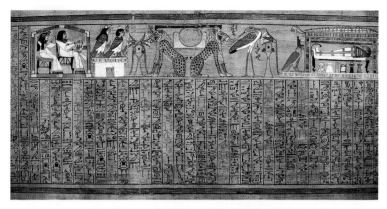

9a. A portion of the "Papyrus of Ani" from Wallis Budge's *The Book of the Dead*, published by Longman & Co. in London in 1899

9b&c. Portions of the "Papyrus of Hu-Neter" (Reign of Seti I, 1306-1290 BC) from Wallis Budge's *The Book of the Dead*, published by Longman & Co. in London in 1899.

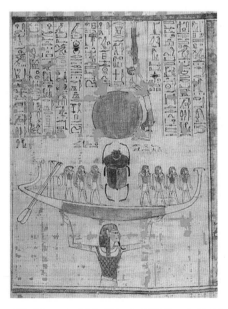

10. A Portion of the "Papyrus of Anhai" (ca 1050 BC, Twenty-First Dynasty) from Wallis Budge's *The Book of the Dead*, published by Longman & Co. in London in 1899.

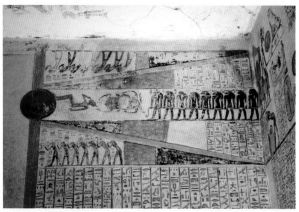

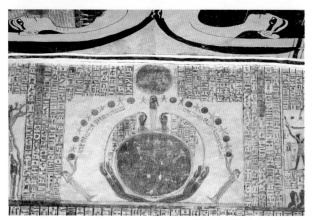

11. The Book of the Dead on the walls of the tomb of Rameses V (1150–1145 BC) and VI (1145-1137 BC). This tomb (number KV9) is situated just behind Tutankhamun's (Tut's) little tomb.

12. Atum and symbols of the origins of life between the two eyes, with the symbol of infinity and temporality (shen), water of life, and the "cup that runneth over."

13a. Depictions of some of the original gods that represent aspects of the Creative Forces.

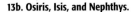

13b. Osiris, Isis, and Nephthys.

14a&b. Queen Nefertiti, originally *Naf-teta*, meaning, "the beauty has come."

15. Pharaoh Tutankhamun's (Tut's) Mask.

16. "Opening the Mouth" to speak in the life
beyond the physical and other preparations.

17a&b. The Soul (Ba) leaving the body.
In 17b we also see the Shadow (*sheut* or
khaibit) at the gate to other realms.

18. The *Shen* held in the talons of the vulture *Nekhbet* on the wall of Hatshepshut's temple. It is the symbol of the "white light" that occurs when eternity (the circle) and temporality (the shaft) are united.

19. Drinking the Water of Life next to the Tree(s) of Life while her soul (*ba*) watches from the mound.

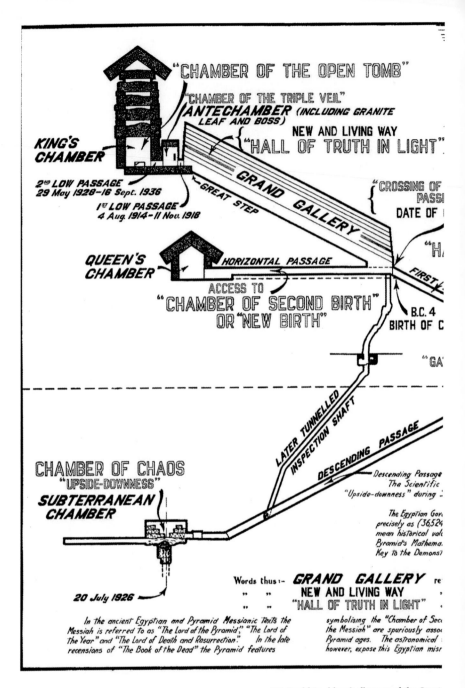

20. David Davidson's diagram of the Great

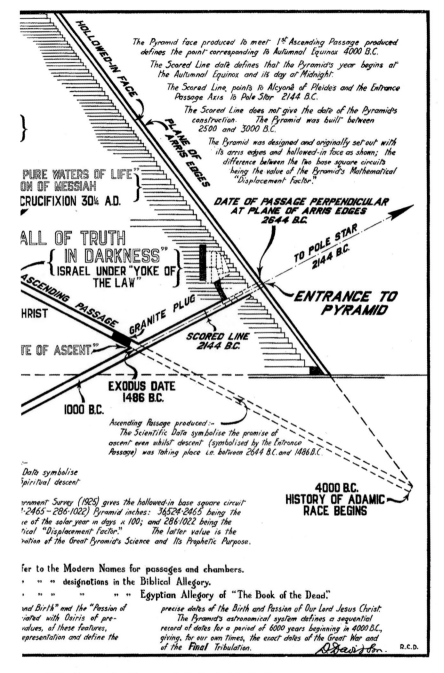

The Pyramid face produced to meet 1st Ascending Passage produced defines the point corresponding to Autumnal Equinox 4000 B.C.

The Scored Line date defines that the Pyramid's year begins at the Autumnal Equinox and its day at Midnight.

The Scored Line, points to Alcyone of Pleides and the Entrance Passage Axis to Pole Star 2144 B.C.

The Scored Line does not give the date of the Pyramid's construction. The Pyramid was built between 2500 and 3000 B.C.

The Pyramid was designed and originally set out with its arris edges and hollowed-in face as shown; the difference between the two base square circuits being the value of the Pyramid's Mathematical "Displacement Factor."

HOLLOWED-IN FACE

PLANE OF ARRIS EDGES

PURE WATERS OF LIFE"
ON OF MESSIAH
CRUCIFIXION 30¼ A.D.

DATE OF PASSAGE PERPENDICULAR
AT PLANE OF ARRIS EDGES
2644 B.C.

ALL OF TRUTH
{ IN DARKNESS"
{ ISRAEL UNDER "YOKE OF
THE LAW"

TO POLE STAR
2144 B.C.

ASCENDING PASSAGE

HRIST

GRANITE PLUG

ENTRANCE TO
PYRAMID

TE OF ASCENT"

SCORED LINE
2144 B.C.

EXODUS DATE
1486 B.C.

1000 B.C.

Ascending Passage produced:-
The Scientific Data symbolise the promise of ascent even whilst descent (symbolised by the Entrance Passage) was taking place i.e. between 2644 B.C. and 1486 B.C.

:-
Data symbolise
Spiritual descent

4000 B.C.
HISTORY OF ADAMIC
RACE BEGINS

ernment Survey (1925) gives the hollowed-in base square circuit
·2465 ~ 286·1022) Pyramid inches: 36,524·2465 being the
te of the solar year in days × 100; and 286·1022 being the
tical "Displacement Factor." The latter value is the
ration of the Great Pyramid's Science and Its Prophetic Purpose.

fer to the Modern Names for passages and chambers.
" " " designations in the Biblical Allegory.
" " " " " " Egyptian Allegory of "The Book of the Dead."
nd Birth" and the "Passion of   precise dates of the Birth and Passion of Our Lord Jesus Christ.
iated with Osiris of pre-   The Pyramid's astronomical system defines a sequential
values, of these features,   record of dates for a period of 6000 years beginning in 4000 B.C.,
epresentation and define the   giving, for our own times, the exact dates of the Great War and
                                                of the Final Tribulation. D. Davidson.

R.C.D.

Pyramid timeline correlated to names in the Book of the Dead.

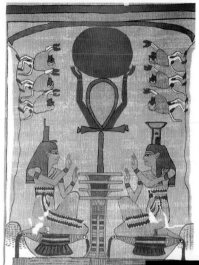

21a&b. The "djed" symbol being honored by Isis (left) and her sister Nephthys (right). 21a shows the ankh of life on top of the djed with the red hands of the "Great Spirit" and the red disk of the "Mind of God."

22. Original entrance to the Great Pyramid forming a double corbeled arch. Notice the recessed triangle in which appears the glyph "Horizon of the Light."

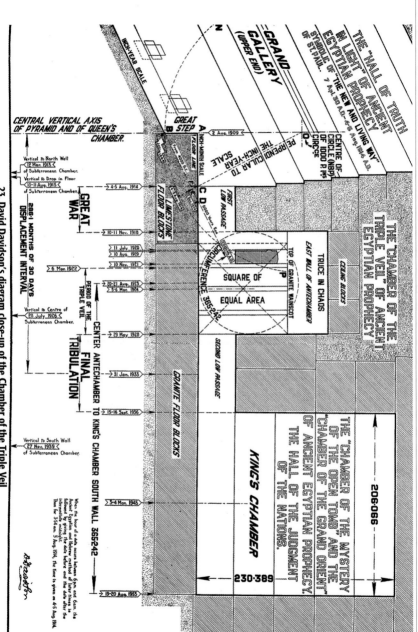

23. David Davidson's diagram close-up of the Chamber of the Triple Veil and the King's Chamber and correlated to modern dates and events.

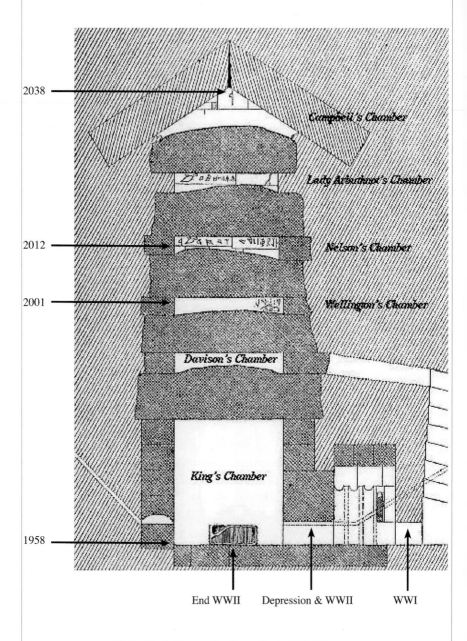

2038

Campbell's Chamber

Lady Arbuthnot's Chamber

2012

Nelson's Chamber

2001

Wellington's Chamber

Davison's Chamber

King's Chamber

1958

End WWII   Depression & WWII   WWI

24. The King's Chamber timeline ending in 2038 at the apex.

not necessarily the *physical* records. As strange as this may seem, according to Cayce, the records are also recorded in consciousness, in the deeper collective mind of humanity, and therefore one could open and study the records anytime by entering deep meditation. Here is an excerpt from one of these strange readings:

> Q: How may I now find those records, or should I wait—or must I wait?
>
> A: You will find the records by that channel as indicated, as these may be obtained *mentally*. As for the physical records—it will be necessary to wait until the full time has come for the breaking up of much that has been in the nature of selfish motives in the world. For, remember, these records were made from the angle of *world* movements. So must thy activities be in the present of the universal approach, but as applied to the individual. Keep the faith. Know that the ability lies within self.   2329-3

When he was asked what changes might be expected in 2038, he replied that a new physical body for incarnating souls will be fully evolved. It will have twelve chakras rather than the seven we currently have. It will be lighter, less dense, and more radiant (perhaps indicating a brighter aura). He said that the New Age will begin at this time and that the prophecy of the pyramid will be fulfilled and over, indicating that there is no more to learn from the pyramid once this year is reached. It will be an age of enlightenment.

As Cayce expressed it in his reading 5750-1, we are close:

> "Yet, as time draws nigh when changes are to come about, there may be the opening of those three places where the records are one, to those that are the initiates in the knowledge of the One God:
>
> "The temple by Iltar will then rise again. Also there will be the opening of the temple or hall of records in Egypt, and those records that were put into the heart of the Atlantean land may also be found there—that have been kept, for those that are of that group.
>
> "The *records* are *one*."

Edgar Cayce's Ancient Timeline

YEAR   **EVENT**

4.6 Billion Years   **Beginning of the Earth Experience.**
"When the morning stars sang before the present together and all the sons and daughters of God shouted for joy announcing the advent of man into material existence." (2441-4)

12 million years   **1st Root Race**
The first soul influx into the ancient Pacific Ocean happened before the present continent of Mu, or Lemuria. The records found in a cave in China referred to this ancient land as the Motherland Mu.

10 Million Years   **2nd Root Race**
The second soul influx into improved bodies began before the present in Mu, or Lemuria.

210,000 BC   **Atlantean Civilization Begins**
Atlantis begins with the influx of souls onto the ancient Atlantic Ocean continent of Atlantis for the purpose of correcting everything that had gone wrong.

106,000 BC   **3rd Root Race**
The third improvement upon a physical form for the souls to inhabit begins. The Logos, Son of God, enters to help all souls. Up to this point bodies have been female and male in one. The Logos divides its two united genders into separate beings, Amilius and Lilith. Lilith is dominant, as are all females at this time. Feminine rule begins around the planet and lasts until the Great Flood. After the Great Flood, the masculine begins to dominant and rule.

50,700 BC   **The first breakup of Atlantis into five islands occurs.**

28,000 BC   **The second breakup of Atlantis happens.**

22,800 BC   **The Great Flood begins.**
God decides to wash the slate clean and begin again (Genesis 6).

12,000 BC   **4th Root Race**
A new and improved body is developed to help souls better evolve through this entrapment in matter. It is the Adamic body. The Logos again enters and separates its genders into Adam and Eve. This pattern occurs in five places on the planet at once: the White Race in the

Caucasus, the Black in the Sudan, Nubia; the Yellow in the Gobi, the
Brown in the eastern portions of the remnant of Mu, the Andes mountain range; and the Red in the remnant of Atlantis.

10,500 BC   New Centers are built.
Most notable are the Giza plateau in Egypt, the Golden Temple in the
Gobi, temples and pyramids in Yucatan, mounds in North America, even
temples that eventually sink are built in Atlantis and Mu. The Giza
monuments, especially the Sphinx and the Great Pyramid, are constructed during this period. The Great Pyramid takes one hundred years
to complete.

10,014 BC   The Final Destruction of Atlantis occurs.
The only remaining island of Poseidia sinks. All remnant groups from
Atlantis have migrated to the shores of North America (today these are
the Iroquois), to the Pyrenees Mountains, (today these are the Basque),
to the Yucatan Peninsula, and to Egypt. Only tiny little islands remain
from Mu's destruction. Many of the Lemurians migrated to Asia, North
and South America, while even some went as far away as India.

He explained that record in the pyramid "is from that as recorded
from the journey to Pyrenees [the escape from sinking Atlantis]; and to
1998 from the death of the Son of Man as a man." (378–14) From Cayce's
perspective, the year 1998 was a "milestone" in the journey of our souls.
It marked the beginning to a New Age, an age of enlightenment and
rapid soul growth. The biblical book of Revelation identifies this age as
being a time when "Satan is bound" and lasting roughly 1,000 years.
Cayce also correlated the beginning of this New Age with a shifting of
the Earth poles, something scientists have recently confirmed. The magnetic poles of the Earth are in the process of shifting, a process that
began around 1998.

NOVA, the PBS television program from WGBH in Boston, reported
startling discoveries about our planet's electromagnetic poles and fields.
The program was titled "Magnetic Storm" and was written and produced by David Sington. The reason this is of interest to us is that Edgar
Cayce predicted that the beginning of the New Age would coincide with
a pole shift. In this NOVA episode, scientists explained that, "2,000 miles
beneath our feet is the Earth's molten core. Here a vast ocean of liquid
iron generates an invisible force, the Earth's magnetic field. It's what

makes our compasses point north. But it does a lot more: it helps to keep the Earth a living planet. Our neighbors, Venus and Mars, have only weak magnetic fields which means that they're unprotected from the deadly radiation sweeping through the solar system. The Earth, on the other hand, exists within a vast magnetic cocoon, a force-field that for billions of years has sheltered us on our journey through space." (29)

But now scientists have made a startling discovery: it seems there's a storm brewing deep within the Earth, a storm that is weakening our vital magnetic shield. Peter Olson at Johns Hopkins University explained that "the Earth's magnetic field has been our protector for millennia, and now, it appears, it's about to go away." (29)

John Shaw of the University of Liverpool explains that, "Pottery acts just like a magnetic tape recorder. It records the Earth's magnetic field when the pottery is first made." (29) The intense heat in the kiln erases all the magnetic regions. But as the pot begins to cool, new magnetic regions form in the magnetite. And as the regions reform, they align with the Earth's magnetic field, just like compass needles. With millions of tiny magnets all pointing in the same general direction, the pot itself becomes slightly magnetic. Once it has cooled, the magnetism is locked in. "So if we take an ancient pot, when it cooled for the first time, it cooled in the Earth's ancient magnetic field and it became magnetized in that field. And of course, if the field's very strong, then the pot's strongly magnetized, and if the field's very weak, then the pot's weakly magnetized," Shaw explained. (29) By examining pottery from prehistory to modern times, Shaw has discovered just how dramatically the field has changed in the last few centuries. "When we plot the results from the ceramics, this is what we see: gentle changes as we come forward in time over twelve thousand years—a gentle rise—and then a rapid fall, as we come towards the present day. The rate of change is higher over the last three hundred years than it has been for any time in the past five thousand. It's going from a strong field down to a weak field, and it's doing it very quickly." (29) In three hundred years the field has fallen 10 percent. And the rate of decline is increasing. In just a few centuries it could be gone altogether.)

For several years now Mt. Kilauea in Hawaii has been continuously erupting. Scientists from the U.S. Geological Survey sample the lava to keep an eye on the volcano. Mike Fuller of the University of Hawaii is interested in the lava because it tells him about the earth's magnetic field. As this lava hits the seawater, it hardens very quickly. As it solidifies and cools, the resultant volcanic rocks are preserving a record of today's magnetic field. But the volcanoes of Hawaii have been erupting, on and off, for millions of years, building up the islands. Every layer of lava contains a record of the magnetic field at the time of that eruption. So the Hawaiian archipelago is a hidden chronicle of the Earth's magnetism, stretching back five and a half million years. That record shows there have been many fluctuations in the Earth's magnetic field, but it contains something else of great significance. When lava cools—as with pottery—magnetic regions form within it. Acting like microscopic compass needles, they record not only how strong the field is, but also in what direction it is pointing. Today the Earth's magnetic field runs from south to north, which is why compass needles point towards the North Pole, and the recent lava flows record a field pointing north. But fifty years ago, when scientists measured the magnetism trapped in older lava samples, they made a startling discovery: the microscopic magnets within the lava were all pointing south. As they examined samples from older and older lava, scientists found more and more reversals; on average, one every 200,000 years. Strangely, there hasn't been a reversal for the past 780,000 years. Fuller believes "we are a bit overdue for a reversal." (29)

In reading 826-1, Cayce indicated that the pole shift would become apparent in 2000 to 2001. The NOVA show revealed that the shift has indeed begun in the South Atlantic Ocean region between Africa and South America. Here the north-south polarity is fluctuating back and forth, weakening the shield against solar radiation. During the pole shift process, the planet's electromagnetic shield will no longer channel the solar winds to our current poles, where few people live. The Northern and Southern lights are a result of radiation moving to the poles. Since radiation causes many problems, the weakening of the shield is a concern. A weak magnetic shield also means that the Northern and Southern lights will be seen all around the planet, even along the equator. It may be a beautiful, wondrous, visionary time for Earth but not a healthy time for many of its inhabitants.

Andrew Coates with the Mullard Space Science Laboratory at the University College London explained, "The sun is a thermonuclear furnace, and this flings off huge amounts of dangerous material in very large explosions. In some cases, it's about the same mass as Mount Everest actually coming towards us. We're lucky on the Earth, we have the magnetic field that deflects the particles and protects us. But if we lost the magnetic field, there would be nothing to stop the radiation bathing the whole of the atmosphere, and the effect would be much more dangerous." (29)

Physicist Gary Glatzmaier at the University of California, Santa Cruz, says that, "it's not going to be catastrophic. It'll be something to be concerned about, but it won't be a catastrophic event. And certainly by the time it happens, civilization will have figured out how to deal with it." (29)

Glatzmaier explains that "the intensity of the magnetic field will be weaker, maybe ten, maybe a hundred times weaker than it is today, which means that more cosmic radiation will get through." (29) Coates explained that, "this basically opens our defenses so that solar and galactic radiation can hit the atmosphere directly. And this means that the radiation at ground level increases as well. This unfortunately means more deaths from cancer. It's roughly 15 per million people per year. That is the amount of deaths we're talking about. And if you multiply that over the whole population of the Earth, that becomes a significant number." (29) But Coates then turned his attention toward one of the positive aspects of a pole shift: "The great thing is that it would be possible to see the aurora (Northern and Southern Lights) just about every night all over the Earth. So in London, for example, we might be able to see great aurora just about every night of the year, shimmering and moving in the sky as the solar wind hits the atmosphere directly, and it glows like a neon light." (29)

Here are two relevant Cayce readings:

> Change, we see, begins in '58 and ends with the changes wrought in the upheavals and the shifting of the poles, as begins then the reign in '98.   378-16

> Q: What great change or the beginning of what change, if any, is
> to take place in the earth in the year 2,000 to 2,001 A.D.?
> A: When there is a shifting of the poles; or a new cycle begins.
>
> 826-8

When asked to explain what some of the characteristics of the New Age would be, Cayce answered: "In the Piscean age, in the center of same, we had the entrance of Emmanuel or God among men, see? What did that mean? The same will be meant by the full consciousness of the ability to communicate with or to be aware of the relationships to the Creative Forces and the uses of same in material environs. This awareness during the era or age in the age of Atlantis and Lemuria or Mu brought what? Destruction to man, and his beginning of the needs of the journey up through that of selfishness. Then, as to what will these be—ONLY those who accept same will even become aware of what's going on about them! How few realize the vibratory forces as create influences from even one individual to another, when they are even in the same vibratory force or influence! And yet ye ask what will the Aquarian age bring in mind, in body, in experience?" (1602-3)

Cayce expressed excitement for this New Age: "that vision of the NEW AGE, the new understanding, the new seeking for the relationships of a Creative Force to the sons of men." (1436-1)

> Q: What can I do to help bring about the New Age?
> A: You will have to practice it in your own life.   5154-1

As much as we identify with planet Earth and our terrestrial life, Edgar Cayce's readings of the Akashic Records and the Universal Consciousness tell a different story. From Cayce's perspective, we are celestial beings, traversing the vast expanse of space in our primal mission to learn more about ourselves and our Creator. Consider this reading, which I've edited for clarity, and focus on the point at hand:

"As an entity passes on from this present time or this solar system, this sun, these forces, it passes through the various spheres—on and on through the EONS of time or space—leading first into that central force known as Arcturus—nearer the Pleiades. Eventually, an entity passes into the inner forces, inner sense, then they may again—after a period of nearly ten thousand years—enter into the earth to make manifest those forces gained in its passage. In entering, the entity takes on those forms that may be known in the dimensions of that plane which it occupies, there being not only three dimensions as of the earth but there may be seven as in Mercury, or four in Venus, or five in Jupiter. There may be only one as in Mars. There may be many more as in those of Neptune, or they may become even as nil—until purified in Saturn's fires." (311-2)

Cayce would begin soul readings for individuals by identifying their planetary and stellar influences, explaining that these were influences because of the souls' journeys through these dimensions prior to incarnating again. He explained: "As the entity moves from sphere to sphere, it seeks its way to the home, to the face of the Creator, the Father, the first cause." (136-8) Cayce identifies the first cause as this: "That the created would be the companion for the Creator." This is the reason we were created, and as a result, the created (our soul) is given opportunities to "show itself to be not only worthy of, but companionable to, the Creator." (5753-1) Since we are talking about the Creator of the entire Cosmos and everything in it, we are celestial star travelers, even though we feel so earthly and terrestrial in our daily lives.

Cayce said that our taking many forms in many different dimensions and spheres helps us to experience the whole of our being and of our Creator's consciousness. He said that "self is lost in that of attaining for itself the nearer and nearer approach that builds in manifested form, whether in the Pleiades, Arcturus, Gemini, or in Earth, in Arcturus, Vulcan, or in Neptune." (136-83) Yet, despite our taking on many "forms" as we manifest ourselves, our true nature is "as light, a ray that does not end, lives on and on, until it becomes one in essence with the source of light." (136-83) This is reminiscent of the ancient Egyptian concept of Ra and how all souls are rays from that Great Light.

9

CONCLUSION

When it comes to human ideas about the ultimate destiny for humanity, we have many. Among them are the alien scenarios. Ugly aliens or deceptively human–looking aliens take over earth, and humanity is enslaved or annihilated. Or pleasing aliens invade Earth and we live together in a technological wonderland. Another is the dark scenario in which humankind falls into decadence in an Urban Hell or Nuclear Wasteland. A popular scenario is how robots and artificial intelligence overtake humanity, and we now work for them. Post–nuclear-war Earth has been a common scenario, though less so since the Cold War ended—but it's making a slight comeback in the scenario of renegade terrorists getting their hands on nukes. Another theme is the utopia scenario in which everyone lives an ideal life of pleasure and ease, though possibly at the expense of excitement and adventure. And there is the evangelical scenario in which God returns when we least expect it to punish the wayward souls, in most cases removing them from the planet. Add the New Agers to the scene and we have God setting up a new kingdom of love and light in which all souls get along while evil is bound and cast into a bottomless pit.

Few scenarios contain the idea that all of humanity will return to heavenly, metaphysical origins, as the ancient Egyptians appear to have believed and devoted so much time training and aiding one another to realize.

Unlike most visions of humanity's future, which are focused on making heaven–on–earth, the ancient Egyptians were ultimately oriented beyond earth. The final achievement was not realized in this world—though good in this life strengthened the next—but rather it was realized in multi–dimensions of nonphysical realms of consciousness and activity.

Now bear with me as we take a metaphysical, mystical tour of ancient thought and the psychic perspectives of the former high priest in Egypt.

The reincarnated Egyptian high priest affirms this mystical destiny of the ancient Egyptians and sees it applicable to all human beings. He even encourages incarnate souls to budget time for metaphysical training, experiences, and growth in nonphysical perception. The returning high priest wanted more time budgeted for deep meditation, conscious dreaming while in sleep (sleep being the shadow of death), and purposeful application of the "Fruits of the Spirit" in daily interaction with others and with oneself. Like the ancient Egyptians, he taught that we are only temporarily terrestrial beings, but we are eternally celestial beings belonging to infinity and eternity, as minds and life forces. When asked how we will ultimately explore space, he answered, "at the speed of thought"; again taking us to a condition of consciousness, not one of physicality. Our bodies were simply not designed for physical space travel. And when it came to the nature of life, the high priest saw a much different dynamic:

> "The study of electrical energies is the basis for finding in a scientific manner the motivative force of animation in matter. But in the study of this activity of electronic energy in man, look for it in the *lower* frequency and not in the ultra. For Life is, and its

manifestations in matter are, of an *electronic* energy.

"Materiality or matter demonstrates and manifests the units of positive and negative energy, or electricity, or God. Life itself is the Creative Force or God, yet its manifestations in man are electrical, or vibratory. Whatever electricity is to man, that's what the power of God is. Man may in the material world use God-force, God-power or electricity, to do man's work or to destroy himself. Know then that the force in nature that is called electrical or electricity is that same force you worship as the Creative or God in action!

"Electricity is life in the nerve force of the body. Impressions produced through the sensory system act on the nervous system of the body. Relays of these are along the stations of ganglia or nerve centers along the spine and in the deeper nervous system. The relays of nerves to the sensory system are through the sympathetics (autonomic system: the sympathetic and the parasympathetic). Those nerves of the cerebrospinal system, or the spinal cord, are in the brain itself and end through the oblongata.

"The liver and the kidneys are the positive and negative poles of a human body, and when one of these becomes overtaxed, the other becomes supercharged in its functioning. Now, as to the activities of the liver and the kidneys, they are as the poles of a generator that are positive and negative in their reaction. The liver is an excretory and a secreting organ. The kidneys are excretory and secreting but in the opposite way and manner. The liver prepares values for the *assimilating*, and necessary elements to produce better assimilation. The functioning of the kidneys is rather to *purify* the circulation by taking from the blood supply infectious forces that are carried off by the slushing of same with the quantities of water taken. See?"

Cayce's discourses included many on the body's spiritual dynamics. He supported and developed further many of the concepts that Eastern religions have taught for thousands of years. According to these ancient schools, many of the body's major systems may be used for *spiritual activity* as well as their more common physical activities. According to

Cayce's insights from his contact with the deeper, collective conscious-ness, the seven major endocrine glands that secrete hormones directly into the bloodstream to keep the body running optimally are a physical portion of the seven spiritual centers that Eastern have been teaching about, the chakras—which literally means spinning "wheel." This aspect of the endocrine glands function can effect significant changes in the vibrations and consciousness of the mind inhabiting a body that has enlivened chakras. The central nervous system, so vital to living in the three-dimensional world, is also a portion of the pathway of the life force through the body called the "kundalini" by Eastern schools. Mov-ing the life force up through the spinal column nerves can raise the vibrations and help the mind perceive at higher levels of consciousness.

Much of this was known in the sacred and often secret temple schools of ancient cultures around the world. For example, the staff carried by the god Mercury (also known as Hermes by the Greeks, Thoth by the Egyptians, and Enoch by the Hebrews) remains today as the emblem of modern medicine, the *caduceus*. But few know its original meaning. It is an excellent emblem for physical healing because it contains the meta-physical structure of the body. The main shaft with the ball at the top is symbolic of the human central nervous system, the cerebrospinal sys-tem: brain and spinal column, with its fluid and nerves producing bio-chemical electricity in the body. The double serpents around this central shaft is symbolic of the autonomic nervous system: a woven complex of nerves and ganglia that innervates the blood vessels, heart, muscles, viscera, and glands from the brain down through the body and controls their involuntary functions. The autonomic system is composed of a sympathetic and parasympathetic division (hence, the two interwoven serpents). The wings at the top of the caduceus symbolize the mind, particularly the power of the mind over the body, mind over matter.

An important but often forgotten teaching in several ancient temple schools dealt with the movement of the life force in the body. It was taught that when the life force flows downward and outward through the body's structures, one becomes fully incarnate and conscious in this world; when the life force flows inward and upward through these same structures, then one moves beyond this reality and becomes conscious of the heavens. Many of the classical schools taught that moving this life force or kundalini was accomplished by using the breath, breathing being of the life force in a living body. The Taoist teacher Liu Hua-yang wrote: "There is a turn upward toward Heaven when the breath is drawn in. When the breath flows out, energy is directed towards the Earth. In two intervals one gathers Sacred Energy."

The body was seen as a temple for the divine, eternal portion of the being who was inhabiting it.

The disciple Paul asked in First Corinthians: "Don't you know that you are a temple of God, and that the Spirit of God dwells in you?" and "Don't you know that your body is a temple of the Holy Spirit which is in you, which you have from God?" In Second Corinthians he comes right out and says it plainly: "We are a temple of the living God; even as God said, 'I will dwell in them, and walk in them; and I will be their God, and they shall be my people.'"

Entering the body temple, raising the energy, enlivening the spiritual centers, and uniting with the source of life was considered essential to experiencing the whole of one's true self in harmony with Creative or God consciousness and eternal life.

Moses, one of the favorites of pharaoh, highly trained in the ways of Egypt, the land of mystery, left pharaoh and the wealth of Egypt because he sensed that there might be more to him than he had realized. He goes out into the desert to find out who he really is and to seek God in a more direct manner. The author of this story is cleverly conveying a deeper truth in the telling of an apparently physical story. He has Moses come upon a deep well in the desert around which seven virgins are standing—certainly a very rare event in the desert. The seven maidens cannot get the life-giving water from the well for themselves and their flocks because other herdsmen keep pushing them away. Moses, one man, drives off all the other herdsmen and waters the seven maidens and their flocks. Then the ladies tell him that they are the daughters of a high priest. Moses goes to the tent of their father, the high priest, and there he eventually marries the eldest daughter, symbolic of bonding with the highest chakra of the seven. After this marriage he hears God in a flaming bush. In the New Testament story the spirit of God in the form of the Holy Spirit comes upon the holy women and the disciples in the form of a tongue of fire over the "bush" of the hair on their heads at the location of the crown chakra. From the flaming bush God teaches Moses to transform his staff into a serpent and the serpent into a power, magical staff. In this allegorical story, Moses could not ascend the mountain and meet God face-to-face until he first gave water to the seven maidens and raised the serpent off the desert floor—symbolic of enlivening the seven spiritual chakras and raising the kundalini energy.

The body's secret structure and some of the techniques for enhancing the life force within us and channeling the life into our lives can be arranged and explained as follows:

Among the first formal documentations of spiritual structures, including energy centers and pathways, was Patanjali's Yoga Sutras, ca 300 BC. He revealed that not only was the human body an excellent device for physical incarnation and activity, it was secretly designed for marvelous metaphysical existence and activity. He taught that there are six centers plus an ultimate luminescence that occurs around the top of the head. These centers are depicted in two ways: as *chakras* (literally, spinning "wheels" of energy) and as *padmas* (literally, "lotuses" of unfolding consciousness). Therefore, one may understand that the spiritual centers are both energy vortexes that generate movement as they are stimulated (as a spinning wheel) and enlightenment complexes that unfold as they grow (as a lotus opens its petals).

Edgar Cayce's psychic discourses correlated these centers with the endocrine glandular system in the body. Whenever we find seven people, places, or things in a classical story, we may correlate them with the seven spiritual centers. For example in the Great Pyramid there are seven layers to the walls in the Grand Gallery and seven rows of ceiling stones above the sarcophagus, five of granite and two of limestone.

Cayce's most mystical example of the secret meaning of sevens is in his interpretation of the many sevens in the Book of Revelation. Cayce correlates the seven churches, seven seals, seven vials, and seven plagues to the cleansing and opening of the seven spiritual centers within a seeker's physical body. He taught that the first ten chapters of this mystical book convey the process and experience of spiritualizing the body temple and the next chapters are the spiritualizing of the mind. The last two chapters are the fulfillment of the promises.

Patanjali identifies three pathways in the body temple. The first two are an interwoven double helix, called *ida* and *pingala*, often represented by double serpents (as in the caduceus). The third is a single path, the *sushumna*, beginning in the lower pelvic area and traveling directly up the body to the top of the head. These pathways correspond to the body's two nervous systems: the sushumna to the central nervous system, with its spinal column and the brain, and the ida and pingala to the deeper autonomic nervous system, with its woven nerves that begin in the lower torso and ascend to the brain. These three pathways act as one. The energy flows through them simultaneously.

Several of the classical mystical concepts and images resemble electrical and electromagnetic theory and devices.

Consider the caduceus, Mercury's staff: a central staff around which two serpents are wound. If the central staff were iron and the serpent coils copper, we would have the basic structure of an electromagnet. Another Egyptian artifact resembling Mercury's staff is the scepter of the goddess Isis. Over seventy of these strange scepters have been found. They are composed of a single shaft around which two copper cobras coil—very similar to Mercury's staff but without the wings. The Hindu central bodily conduit of energy, the sushumna, is surrounded by the woven coils of ida and pingala.

The idea of raising one's physical and mental vibrations, one's biochemical energy, suggests the stimulation of electrons and the movement of charged particles, resulting in energy output, field generation, luminous radiation, heating effects, and other manifestations so typical of electrical and electromagnetic activity. And since the chakras are associated with the seven major endocrine glands, the hormonal messages in the blood stream may be altered as well. Mystics often describe their altered experiences as generating heat, luminescence, movement, liberation, levitation, and expansion—all characteristics of electricity and magnetism. Modern day quantum electrodynamics (QED) theorizes that electric fields are simply clouds of *virtual* photons, and that these photons are particles that aren't even real in the sense of true matter or physicality. They come from nowhere, yet even a single-charged particle has a cloud of virtual photons around it. This virtual photon cloud is akin to the electric field of energy and light that the mystics describe and correlate to their chakras and kundalini energy, as well as to their higher mental state when in deep meditation. The ancient mystics and the modern physicists are sounding strangely similar.

Some science is pushing into virtual realities and subtler yet powerful energies, as were the ancient Egyptians in their transitioning from earthly manifestation to celestial existence in the realms of the Netherworld and beyond. This appears to be the prophecy conveyed in the Great Pyramid timeline and its correlation to the *Egyptian Book of the Dead*. And it may be humanity's ultimate destiny.

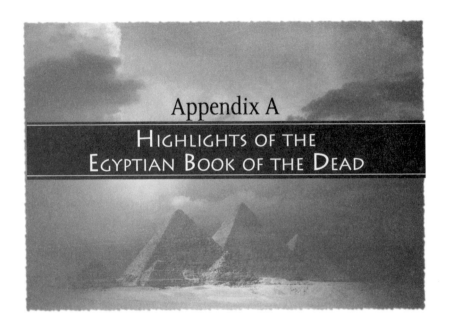

Appendix A

HIGHLIGHTS OF THE EGYPTIAN BOOK OF THE DEAD

The following are selections from the whole of the *Egyptian Book of the Dead* that provide us with a perspective into the transitional passage from earthly existence and awareness to transcendental existence and consciousness.

Although the Egyptian *Ani* is named here, the original text allowed for Ani's name to be replaced by the name of any other person who was going through this transition. And whoever was named here would also have the name "Osiris" added to his or her name, indicating his or her existence in the realms of Osiris, to wit: the Netherworld. Thus, Ani is called Osiris Ani; sometimes he (and any one in his role) is simply called Osiris.

In this context the Egyptian names of physical places in ancient Egypt are actually realms of the heavenly world. Every place, power, activity, and person in this world has its heavenly reflection. For example, the city of Heliopolis is also the mythological Annu; in the context of the

Egyptian Book of Dead, Annu is the capital of the heavenly metaphysical world. And though Hensu was a city in Egypt that usurped the throne for a short time, thus representing rebellion, and was known as the City of Crocodiles, it now represents the energies of the lower nature or the root chakra with ida and pingala, the so-called "double nest" and "double cobras" (double *uraei*), which have now been turned toward heavenly obedience and service.

Sir Wallis Budge originally translated the text used here. I have changed Budge's biblical language style (all the *-eths*: goeth, cometh, and the like) to modern language. I have also replaced or explained Egyptian names and terms with their literal or mystical meaning. I have also replaced British spelling with American spelling; for example, *favour* with "favor" and *honour* with "honor."

The Weighing of the Heart

THE PRAYER OF ANI: My heart, my mother; my heart, my mother! My heart whereby I came into being! May not stand up to oppose me at [my] judgment, may there be no opposition to me in the presence of the Great Chiefs (*Tchatchau*, which Budge explains in his book *Egyptian Heaven and Hell* are the "recording angels" who keep Osiris' register of all the souls and godlings); may there be no parting of you from me in the presence of him that keeps the Balance! You are my KA, which dwells in my body; the god "Lord of the House of Sweet Light and Governor of the House of Life" (*Khnemu*) who knits together and strengthens my limbs. May you come forth into the place of happiness whither we go. May the "stellar princes" (*Sheniu* officials), who make the conditions of the lives of men, not cause my name to stink, and may no lies be spoken against me in the presence of the God. Let it be satisfactory unto us, and let the Listener god be favorable unto us, and let there be joy of heart (to us) at the weighing of words. Let not that which is false be uttered against me before the Great God, the Lord of West and Land of the Dead (Amentet, this Lord is a goddess). Verily, how great shall you be when you rise in triumph.

THE SPEECH OF THOTH: Thoth (the god who records the weighing of the heart), the judge of right and truth of the Great Company of the

Gods who are in the presence of Osiris, says: Hear you this judgment. The heart of Osiris has in very truth been weighed, and his Heart-soul has borne testimony on his behalf; his heart has been found right by the trial in the Great Balance. There has not been found any wickedness in him; he has not wasted the offerings that have been made in the temples; he has not committed any evil act; and he has not set his mouth in motion with words of evil while he was upon earth.

SPEECH OF THE DWELLER IN THE EMBALMMENT CHAMBER (Anubis): Pay good heed, O righteous Judge to the Balance to support [the testimony] thereof. Variant: Pay good heed to the weighing in the Balance of the heart of the Osiris, the singing-woman of Amen, Anhai (a good chantress that helped souls meet their loved ones), whose word is truth, and place you in her heart in the seat of truth in the presence of the Great God.

THE SPEECH OF THE GODS: The Great Company of the Gods says to Thoth who dwells in the city of Thoth (*Khemenu*): That which comes forth from your mouth shall be declared true. The Osiris the scribe Ani, whose word is true, is holy and righteous. He has not committed any sin, and he has done no evil against us. The devourer Am-mit (the little beast who eats hearts that are too heavy to rise into heaven) shall not be permitted to prevail over him. Meat offerings and admittance into the presence of the god Osiris shall be granted unto him, together with an abiding habitation in the Field of Offerings (*Sekhet-hetepet*), as unto the Followers of Horus.

THE SPEECH OF HORUS TO OSIRIS IN INTRODUCING ANI TO HIM: Horus, the son of Isis, says: I have come to you, O Un-Nefer (one that makes beauty and heaven appear), and I have brought unto you the Osiris Ani. His heart is righteous, and it has come forth from the Balance; it has not sinned against any god or any goddess. Thoth has weighed it according to the decree pronounced unto him by the Company of the Gods, and it is most true and righteous. Grant you that cakes and ale may be given unto him, and let him appear in the presence of the god Osiris, and let him be like unto the Followers of Horus forever and ever.

THE SPEECH OF ANI: And the Osiris Ani says: Behold, I am in your presence, O Lord of the West and the Land of the Dead (goddess *Amentet*).

There is no sin in my body. I have not spoken that which is not true knowingly, nor have I done anything with a false heart. Grant you that I may be like unto those favored ones who are in your following, and that I may be an Osiris greatly favored of the beautiful god, and beloved of the Lord of the Two Lands (Atum or Tem), I who am a veritable royal scribe who loves you, Ani, whose word is true before the god Osiris.

HERE BEGIN THE PRAISES AND GLORIFYINGS OF COMING OUT FROM AND OF GOING INTO THE GLORIOUS KHERT-NETER (NETHERWORLD–DIVINE), WHICH IS IN THE BEAUTI-FUL AMENTET (LAND OF THE DEAD), OF COMING FORTH BY DAY IN ALL THE FORMS OF EXISTENCE WHICH IT MAY PLEASE THE DECEASED TO TAKE, OF PLAYING AT DRAUGHTS, OF SIT-TING IN THE SEH HALL, AND OF APPEARING AS A LIVING SOUL:

The Osiris the scribe Ani says after he has arrived in his haven of rest; now it is good for [a man] to recite [this work whilst he is] upon earth, for then all the words of Atum (Budge always translates this god's name as *Tem*—remember, this is the god of gods, the original creator of all) come to pass: "I am the god Atum in rising. I am the Only One. I came into existence in the Water One (*Nu*, the primordial "sea" of dark infinity). I am Ra who rose in the beginning, the ruler of this [creation] (and the light that penetrated the infinite darkness)."

[Now a series of "Who is this?" questions are asked and answered.]

Who is this?

"It is Ra, when at the beginning he rose in the city of Crocodiles (*Hensu*, symbolizing the lower, rebellious forces), crowned like a king for his coronation. The Pillars of the god Shu were not as yet created, when he was upon the steps of him that dwells in the city of Thoth (Khemenu). "I am the Great God who created himself, even the primordial sea (*Nu*), who made his names to become the Company of the Gods as gods."

Who is this?

"It is Ra, the creator of the names of his limbs, which came into being in the form of the gods who are in the train of Ra. 'I am he who cannot be repulsed among the gods.'"

Who is this?

"It is Atum (Temu), the dweller in his disk, but others say that it is Ra when he rises in the eastern horizon of the sky. 'I am Yesterday, I know Today.'"

Who is this?

"Yesterday is Osiris (darkness and death), and Today is Ra (light and life), when he shall destroy the enemies of the "Lord to the Uttermost Limit" (*Neb-er-tcher*), and when he shall establish as prince and ruler his son Horus. 'Others, however, say that Today is Ra, on the day when we commemorate the festival of the meeting of the dead Osiris with his father Ra, and when the battle of the gods was fought, in which Osiris, the Lord of the West and the Land of the Dead (goddess Amentet), was the leader.'"

What is this?

"It is Amentet, [that is to say] the creation of the souls of the gods when Osiris was leader in the hidden place (*Set-Amentet*). 'Others, however, say that it is the Amentet that Ra has given unto me; when any god comes he must rise up and fight for it. I know the god who dwells therein.'"

Who is this?

"It is Osiris. Others, however, say that his name is Ra, and that the god who dwells in Amentet (Land of the Dead) is the phallus of Ra (the phallus rises in the darkness as the Sun rises), wherewith he had union with himself. 'I am the Benu bird which is in the City of the Sun (*Anu*). I am the keeper of the volume of the Tablet of Destiny of the things which have been made, and of the things which shall be made.'"

Who is this?

"It is Osiris. 'Others, however, say that it is the dead body of Osiris, and yet others say that it is the excrement of Osiris. The things that have been made and the things that shall be made refer to the dead body of Osiris. Others again say that the things that have been made are Eternity, and the things that shall be made are Everlastingness, and that Eternity is the Day, and Everlastingness the Night. I am the god Chief of Heaven (*Menu*, also *Min*; a pre–dynastic sky–god whose symbol was a thunderbolt) in his coming forth; may his two plumes be set on my head for me.'"

Who is this?

"The Chief of Heaven (Menu) is Horus, the Advocate of his father [Osiris], and his coming forth means his birth. The two plumes on his head are Isis (goddess of magic, motherhood, and "Mother of the Universe") and Nephthys ("Friend of the Dead" and goddess of divine help and protection), when these goddesses go forth and set themselves thereon, and when they act as his protectors, and when they provide that which his head lacks. 'Others, however, say that the two plumes are the two exceedingly large *uraei* (cobras, as in kundalini and the double of ida and pingala) which are upon the head of their father Atum (Tem), and there are yet others who say that the two plumes which are upon the head of Menu are his two eyes. The Osiris the scribe Ani, whose word is true, the registrar of all the offerings which are made to the gods, rises up and comes into his city.'"

What is this [city]?

"It is the horizon of his father Atum (Tem). I have made an end of my shortcomings, and I have put away my faults."

What is this?

"It is the cutting of the navel string of the body of the Osiris the scribe Ani, whose word is true before all the gods, and all his faults are driven out.

What is this?

"It is the purification [of Osiris] on the day of his birth. 'I am purified in my great double nest which is in the city of Crocodiles (*Hensu*, symbolizing the root chakra, the double nest is likely ida and pingala) on the day of the offerings of the followers of the Great God who dwells therein.'"

What is the "great double nest"?

"The name of one nest is 'Millions of years,' and 'Great Green [Sea]' [in Mayan, *Yax Ha*, "Green Water"] is the name of the other, that is to say 'Lake of Natron' and 'Lake of Salt' [Again, these appear to be the complementary qualities of metaphysical sources and forces. Natron is actually a type of salt, so the two names are somewhat redundant.] 'Others, however, say the name of the one is 'Guide of Millions of Years,' and that

'Great Green Lake' is the other. Yet others say that 'Begetter of Millions of Years' is the name of one, and 'Great Green Lake' is the name of the other. Now, as concerning the Great God who dwells therein, it is Ra himself. "I pass over the way; I know the head of the Island of Maati [truth]."

What is this?

"It is Ra–stau [the vast, etheric plain, which the Giza Plateau symbolizes in physicality], that is to say, it is the gate to the South of Nerutef (realm of the recording angels, the Tchatcha Chiefs), and it is the Northern Gate of the Domain (Tomb of the god). 'Now, as concerning the Island of Maati (Truth), it is Abtu (etheric Abydos, the most holy of holy places). Others, however, say that it is the way by which Father Atum (Tem) travels when he goes forth to Field of Rushes (Sekhet–Aaru), [the place] which produces the food and sustenance of the gods who are [in] their shrines. 'Now the Gate Tchesert (Holy Land of the Netherworld) is the Gate of the Pillars of Shu (emptiness, air), that is to say, the Northern Gate of the Netherworld (Duat, Tuat). Others, however, say that the Gate of Tchesert is the two leaves of the door through which the god Atum (Tem) passes when he goes forth to the eastern horizon of the sky. *O you gods who are in the presence [of Osiris], grant to me your arms, for I am the god who shall come into being among you.*'" [This statement and others clearly indicate that the ancient Egyptians believed all beings could become gods among the Company of Gods, or Godlings, children and ultimately companions of the One Creator God.]

Who are these gods?

"They are the drops of blood which came forth from the phallus of Ra [Light piecing the darkness] when he went forth to perform his own mutilation [Blood was life not sperm, and the sacrifice of one's life for another was and is the ultimate express of selfless love. Ra's wound was quickly healed by Thoth]. These drops of blood sprang into being under the forms of the gods Hu and Sa [representing *expression* (Hu) and *perception* (Sa or Sia)], who are in the bodyguard of Ra, and who accompany the god Atum (Tem) daily and every day. 'I, Osiris the scribe Ani, whose word is truth, have filled for you the *utchat* (the Eye of Ra or of Horus), when it had suffered extinction on the day of the combat of the Two Fighters (Horus and Set)."

What was this combat?

It was the combat that took place on the day when Horus [the higher mind and thought of others' needs] fought with Set [the lower mind and self-seeking selfishness], during which Set threw filth in the face of Horus, and Horus crushed the genitals of Set [stopping the lower self from generating more thoughts and urges of selfishness]. The filling of the *utchat* (the Eye of Horus) Thoth performed with his own fingers. 'I remove the thunder-cloud from the sky when there is a storm with thunder and lightning therein.'"

What is this?

"This storm was the raging of Ra at the thunder-cloud which [Set] sent forth against the Right Eye of Ra (the Sun). Thoth removed the thunder-cloud from the Eye of Ra, and brought back the Eye living, healthy, sound, and with no defect in it to its owner. 'Others, however, say that the thunder-cloud is caused by sickness in the Eye of Ra [in this case, likely means the Sun], which weeps for its companion Eye (the Moon); at this time Thoth cleanses the Right Eye of Ra. 'I behold Ra who was born yesterday from the thighs of the goddess Mehurt [spiritual river of heaven]; his strength is my strength, and my strength is his strength.'"

Who is this?

"Mehurt is the great Celestial Water, but others say that Mehurt is the image of the Eye of Ra at dawn at his birth daily. '[Others, however, say that] Mehurt is the *utchat* [eye] of Ra. Now Osiris the scribe Ani, whose word is truth, is a very great one among the gods who are in the following of Horus; they say that he is the prince who loves his lord.'"

Who are the gods who are in the train of Horus?

"[They are] Kesta, Hapi, Taumutef, and Qebhsenuf [godly forces that cleanse one of all evil and error]. 'Homage to you, O you lords of right and truth, you sovereign princes (Tchatcha, the recording angels) who [stand] round about Osiris, who utterly do away with sins and offenses, and who are in the following of the goddess Hetepsekhus (the eye of Ra), grant you that I may come unto you. Destroy you all the faults that are within me, even as you did for the Seven Spirits who are among the followers of their lord Sepa (a god of the underworld associated with centipedes and bug bites). Anpu (Anubis) appointed to them their places on the day [when he said unto them], *Come you hither.*'"

Who are the "lords of right and truth"?

"The lords of right and truth are Thoth and Astes (the moon aspect of Thoth), the Lord of Land of the Dead (Amentet, a goddess). The Tchatcha (recordkeeping angels) round about Osiris are Kesta, Hapi, Tuamutef, and Qebhsenuf [godly forces that cleanse one of all evil and error], and they are also round about the Constellation of the Thigh (the Great Bear), in the northern sky. Those who do away utterly sins and offenses, and who are in the following of the goddess Hetepsekhus (the eye of Ra in the sense of "seeing everything" in this context), are the god Sebek (son of selfishness who mated with earthiness and lurks under the surface of consciousness waiting to pull innocence into rolling of emotions, thereby numbing higher consciousness] and his associates who dwell in the water. The goddess Hetepsekhus is the Eye of Ra. 'Others, however, say that it is the flame which accompanies Osiris to burn up the souls of his enemies. As concerning all the faults which are in Osiris, the registrar of the offerings which are made unto all the gods, Ani, whose word is truth, [these are all the offences which he has committed against the Lords of Eternity] since he came forth from his mother's womb. As concerning the Seven Spirits who are Kesta, Hapi, Tuamutef, Qebhsenuf, Maa-atef, Kheribeqef and Heru-khenti-en-ariti, these did Anubis appoint to be protectors of the dead body of Osiris. Others, however, say that he set them round about the holy place of Osiris. Others say that the Seven Spirits [which were appointed by Anubis] were Netcheh-netcheh, Aatqetqet, Nertanef-besef-khenti-hehf, Aq-her-ami-unnut-f, Tesher-ariti-ami-Het-anes, Ubes-her-per-em-khetkhet, and Maaem-kerh-annef-em-hru. The chief of the Tchatcha (sovereign princes and recordkeeping angels) who is in Naarutef is Horus, the Advocate of his father. As concerning the day wherein [Anubis said to the Seven Spirits], *Come you hither,* [the allusion here] is to the words *Come you hither,* which Ra spoke unto Osiris.'"

The Seven Arits

The Seven Arits are divisions of *Sekhet Aaru,* which are seven regions in the "Elysian Fields," which are the final resting places of the souls, unless they deserve Hades. This is the realm Asar or Osiris (Asar or Usar is a Greek corruption of Osiris). In the Seven Arits are gates and each gate has three attendants: 1. *gatekeeper*, 2. *watcher* (who announces the arrival of each sojourner), and 3. *herald* (who announces the name of each sojourner). The attendants have names that are *hekau*, meaning evocative, power sounds. Saying these names grants the initiate access through the seven regions, which may well be compared to the seven lotuses of spiritual consciousness.

The attendants for each gate are:

Arit	Gatekeeper	Watcher	Herald
1	Upside Down of Face	Eavesdropper	Roaring Voice
2	Open Countenance	Seqet Face	Glowing
3	Eater of Foulness	Alert of Face	Curser
4	Hostile of Face	Perceptive	Crocodile Repeller
5	Existing on Maggots	Fame Dweller	Hippopotamus Face
6	Raging of Voice	Face Remover	Keen of Face
7	Prevailer over Knives	Strident of Voice	Rebuffer of Insurgents

The First Arit

The name of the Doorkeeper is Upside Down of Face [Sekhet-her-asht-aru]. The name of the Watcher is Eavesdropper [Smetti]. The name of the Herald is Roaring Voice [Hakheru]. The Osiris Ani, whose word is truth, shall say when he comes unto the First Arit: "I am the mighty one who creates his own light. I have come unto you, O Osiris, and, purified from that which defiles you, I adore you. Lead on. Name not the name of Ra–stau to me. Homage to you, O Osiris, in your might and in your strength in Ra–stau. Rise up and conquer, O Osiris, in Abydos (Abtu). You go round about heaven, you sail in the presence of Ra, you look upon all the beings who have knowledge. Hail, Ra, you who goes round about in the sky, I say, O Osiris in truth, that I am the Sahu (Soul–body) of the god, and I beseech you not to let me be driven away, nor to be cast upon the wall of blazing fire. Let the way be opened in Ra–stau, let the pain of the Osiris be relieved, embrace that which the Balance has weighed, let a path be made for the Osiris in the Great Valley, and let the Osiris have light to guide him on his way."

The Second Arit

The name of the Doorkeeper is Open Countenance [Unhat]. The name of the Watcher is Seqet Face [Seqt– her]. The name of the Herald is Glowing [Ust]. The Osiris Ani, whose word is truth, shall say [when he comes to this Arit]: "He sits to carry out his heart's desire, and he weighs words as the Second of Thoth. The strength which protects Thoth humbles the hidden Maati gods, who feed upon Maat [Truth] during the years of their lives. I offer up my offerings [to him] at the moment when he makes his way. I advance, and I enter on the path. O grant you that I may continue to advance, and that I may attain to the sight of Ra, and of those who offer up [their] offerings."

The Third Arit

The name of the Doorkeeper is Eater of Foulness [Unem-hauatu-ent-pehui]. The name of the Watcher is Alert of Face [Seres-her]. The name of the Herald is Curser [Aa]. The Osiris the scribe Ani, whose word is truth, shall say [when he comes to this Arit]: "I am he who is hidden in the great deep. I am the Judge of the Rehui [between Horus and Set, meaning Good and Evil], I have come and I have done away the offensive thing that was upon Osiris. I tie firmly the place on which he stands, coming forth from the Urt [celestial waters]. I have established things in Abtu, I have opened up a way through Ra–stau, and I have relieved the pain that was in Osiris. I have balanced the place whereon he stands, and I have made a path for him; he shines brilliantly in Ra–stau."

The Fourth Arit

The name of the Doorkeeper is Hostile of Face [Khesef-her-asht-kheru]. The name of the Watcher is Perceptive [Seres-tepu]. The name of the Herald Crocodile Repeller is [Khesef-at]. The Osiris the scribe Ani, whose word is truth, shall say [when he comes to this Arit]: "I am the Bull, the son of the ancestress of Osiris. O grant you that his father, the Lord of his god-like companions, may bear witness on his behalf. I have weighed the guilty in judgment. I have brought unto his nostrils the life that is ever lasting. I am the son of Osiris, I have accomplished the journey, I have advanced in Khert-Neter [Divine Netherworld]."

The Fifth Arit

The name of the Doorkeeper is Existing on Maggots [Ankhf-em-fent]. The name of the Watcher is Fame Dweller [Shabu]. The name of the Herald is Hippopotamus Face [Teb-her-kha-kheft]. The Osiris the scribe Ani, whose word is truth, shall say [when he comes to this Arit]: "I have brought unto you the jawbone in Ra-stau. I have brought unto you your backbone in Anu [Heavenly City of the Sun]. I have gathered together his manifold members therein. I have driven back Apep [lower-nature serpent power that distracts one] for you. I have spit upon the wounds [in his body]. I have made myself a path among you. I am the Aged One among the gods. I have made offerings to Osiris. I have defended him with the word of truth. I have gathered together his bones, and have collected all his members."

The Sixth Arit

The name of the Doorkeeper is Raging of Voice [Atek-tau-kehaq-kheru]. The name of the Watcher is Face Remover [An-her]. The name of the Herald is Keen of Face [Ates-her-(ari)-she]. The Osiris the scribe Ani, whose word is truth, shall say [when he comes to this Arit]: "I have come daily, I have come daily. I have made myself a way. I have advanced over that which was created by Anpu (Anubis). I am the Lord of the Urrt Crown [an elaborate plumed crown]. I am the possessor [of the knowledge of] the words of magical power, I am the Avenger according to law, I have avenged [the injury to] his Eye. I have defended Osiris. I have accomplished my journey. The Osiris Ani advances with you with the word which is truth."

The Seventh Arit

The name of the Doorkeeper is Prevailer over Knives [Sekhmet-em-tsu-sen]. The name of the Watcher is Strident of Voice [Aa-maa-kheru]. The name of the Herald is Rebuffer of Insurgents [Khesef-khemi]. The

Osiris the scribe Ani, whose word is truth, shall say [when he comes to this Arit]: "I have come unto you, O Osiris, being purified from foul emissions. You go round about heaven, you see Ra, you see the beings who have knowledge. [Hail], you, ONE! Behold, you are in the Sektet Boat ["the barque (boat) of millions of years"] which traverses the heavens. I speak what I will to his Sahu (Soul-body). He is strong, and comes into being even [as] he speaks. You meet him face to face. Prepare you for me all the ways which are good [and which lead] to you."

RUBRIC: If [these] words be recited by the spirit when he shall come to the Seven Arits, and as he enters the doors, he shall neither be turned back nor repulsed before Osiris, and he shall be made to have his being among the blessed spirits, and to have dominion among the ancestral followers of Osiris. If these things be done for any spirit he shall have his being in that place like a lord of eternity in one body with Osiris, and at no place shall any being contend against him.

The Chapter of Not Dying a Second Time

The Osiris Ani, whose word is truth, says: Hail, Thoth! What is it that has happened to the children of Nut? They have waged war, they have upheld strife, they have done evil, they have created the fiends, they have made slaughter, they have caused trouble; in truth, in all their doings the strong have worked against the weak. Grant, O might of Thoth, that that which the god Atum (Tem) has decreed [may it be done!] And you regard not evil, nor are you provoked to anger when they bring their years to confusion, and throng in and push in to disturb their months. For in all that they have done unto you they have worked iniquity in secret. I am thy writing-palette, O Thoth, and I have brought unto you thine ink-jar. I am not of those who work iniquity in their secret places; let not evil happen unto me.

The Osiris the scribe Ani, whose word is truth, says: Hail, Temu! What manner of land is this unto which I have come? It has not water, it has not air; it is depth unfathomable, it is black as the blackest night, and men wander helplessly therein. In it a man cannot live in quietness of heart; nor may the longings of love be satisfied therein. But let the state of the Spirit-souls be given unto me instead of water and air, and the satisfying of the longings of love, and let quietness of heart be given unto me instead of cakes and ale. The god Atum (Tem) has decreed that I shall see your face, and that I shall not suffer from the things that pain you. May every god transmit unto you his throne for millions of years. Your throne has descended unto your son Horus, and the god Atum (Tem) has decreed that your course shall be among the holy princes. In truth he shall rule from your throne, and he shall be heir to the throne of the Dweller in the fiery Lake [Neserser, a mythical lake within which are seven hidden circles of cleansing flames]. In truth it has been decreed that in me he shall see his likeness, and that my face shall look upon the face of the Lord Atum (Tem). How long then have I to live? It is decreed that you shall live for millions of years, a life of millions of years [then return into the womb of Infinite Mother Creator (Iusaaset), silent and still again]. Let it be granted to me to pass on to the holy princes, for indeed, I have done away all the evil which I committed, from the time when this earth came into being from Nu, when it sprang from the watery abyss even as it was in the days of old. I am Fate and Osiris, I have made my transformations into the likeness of divers serpents. Man knows not, and the gods cannot behold the two-fold beauty which I have made for Osiris, the greatest of the gods. I have given unto him the region of the dead. And, verily, his son Horus is seated upon the throne of the Dweller in the fiery Lake [Neserser], as his heir. I have made him to have his throne in the Boat of Millions of Years. Horus is established upon his throne [among his] kinsmen, and he has all that is with him. Verily, the Soul of Set, which is greater than all the gods, has departed. Let it be granted to me to bind his soul in fetter in the Boat of the God, when I please, and let him hold the Body of the God in fear. O my father Osiris, you hast done for me that which your father Ra did for you. Let me abide upon the earth permanently. Let me keep possession of my throne. Let my heir be strong. Let my tomb, and my friends who are upon the earth, flourish. Let my enemies be given over to destruction, and to the shackles of the goddess Serq [another aspect of Isis]. I am your son. Ra is my father. On me likewise you hast conferred life, strength, and health. Horus is established upon his tomb. Grant you that the days of my life may come unto worship and honor.

RUBRIC: This Chapter shall be recited over a figure of Horus, made of lapis-lazuli, which shall be placed on the neck of the deceased. It is a protection upon earth, and it will secure for the deceased the affection of men, gods, and the Spirit-souls that are perfect. Moreover it acts as a spell in Khert-Neter (Netherworld-Divine), but it must be recited by you on behalf of the Osiris Ra, regularly and continually millions of times.

Entering into the Hall of Maati to Praise Osiris Khenti-amenti.

The Osiris the scribe Ani, whose word is truth, says: I have come unto you. I have drawn nigh to behold your beauties (your beneficent goodness). My hands are [extended] in adoration of your name of *Maat* [Truth]. I have come. I have drawn nigh unto [the place where] the cedar-tree exists not, where the acacia tree doth not put forth shoots, and where the ground produces neither grass nor herbs. Now I have entered into the habitation that is *hidden*, and I hold converse with Set [god of chaos]. My protector advanced to me, covered was his face . . . on the hidden things. He entered into the house of Osiris, he saw the hidden things which were therein. The Tchatchau Chiefs of the Pylons were in the form of Spirits. The god Anpu spoke unto those about him with the words of a man who comes from Ta-mera, saying, "He knows our roads and our towns. I am reconciled unto him. When I smell his odor it is even as the odor of one of you." And I say unto him: I the Osiris Ani, whose word is truth, in peace, whose word is truth, have come. I have drawn nigh to behold the Great Gods. I would live upon the propitiatory offerings [made] to their Doubles. I would live on the borders [of the territory of] the Soul, the Lord of Tetu. He shall make me to come forth in the form of a Benu bird, and to hold converse [with him]. I have been in the stream [to purify myself]. I have made offerings of incense. I betook myself to the Acacia Tree of the [divine] Children. I lived in Abu in the House of the goddess Satet. I made to sink in the water the boat of the enemies. I sailed over the lake [in the temple] in the Neshmet Boat. I have looked upon the Sahu of Kamur. I have been in Tetu. I have held my peace. I have made the god to be master of his legs. I have been in the House of Teptuf. I have seen him, that is the Governor of the

Hall of the God. I have entered into the House of Osiris and I have removed the head-coverings of him that is therein. I have entered into Rasta, and I have seen the Hidden One who is therein. I was hidden, but I found the boundary. I journeyed to Nerutef, and he who was therein covered me with a garment. I have myrrh of women, together with the shenu powder of living folk. Verily he (Osiris) told me the things which concerned himself. I said: Let your weighing of me be even as we desire.

And the Majesty of Anpu shall say unto me, "Knowest you the name of this door, and canst you tell it?" And the Osiris the scribe Ani, whose word is truth, in peace, whose word is truth, shall say, "Khersek-Shu" is the name of this door. And the Majesty of the god Anpu shall say unto me, "Knowest you the name of the upper leaf, and the name of the lower leaf?" [And the Osiris the scribe Ani] shall say: "Neb-Maat-heri-retiu- f" is the name of the upper leaf and "Neb-pehti-thesu-menment" [is the name of the lower leaf. And the Majesty of the god Anpu shall say], "Pass on, for you hast knowledge, O Osiris the scribe, the assessor of the holy offerings of all the gods of Thebes Ani, whose word is truth, the lord of loyal service [to Osiris]."

The Book of Making Perfect the Ahku [Also Khu Akh, Ikhu]

This is the book of making perfect the Ahku [Star Being] in the heart of Ra, of making him to have the mastery before Atum (Tem), of magnifying him before Osiris, of making him mighty before Khent-Land of the Dead (Amentet), and of setting awe of him before the Company of the Gods. It shall be recited on the day of the New Moon, on the sixth day festival, on the fifteenth day festival, on the festival of Uak, on the festival of Thoth, on the Birthday of Osiris, on the festival of Menu, on the night of Heker, [during] the Mysteries of the Tuat, during the celebration of the Mysteries in Akertet, at the smiting of the emissions, at the passage of the Funerary Valley, [and] the Mysteries . . . [The recital thereof] will make the heart of the Khu to flourish and will make long his strides, and will make him to advance, and will make his face bright, and will make it to penetrate to the God. Let no man witness [the recital] except the king and the Kherheb priest, but the servant who comes to minister outside shall not see it. Of the Khu for whom this Book shall be recited, his soul shall come forth by day with the living, he shall have power among the gods, and it will make him irresistible for ever and ever. These gods shall go round about him, and shall acknowledge him. He shall be one of them. [This Book] shall make him to know how he came into being in the beginning. This Book is indeed a veritable mystery. Let no stranger anywhere have knowledge of it. Do not speak about it to any man. Do not repeat it. Let no [other] eye see it. Let no [other] ear hear it. Let no one see it except [thyself] and him who taught [it to you]. Let not the multitude [know of it] except thyself and the beloved friend of your heart. You shall do this book in the seh chamber on a cloth painted with the stars in color all over it. It is indeed a mystery. The dwellers in the swamps of the Delta and everywhere there shall not know it. It shall provide the Akhu (Khu) with celestial food upon in Khert-Neter (Netherworld-Divine). It shall supply his Heart-soul with food upon earth. It shall make him to live forever. No [evil] thing shall have the master over him.

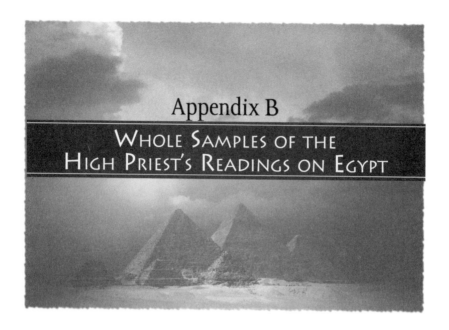

Appendix B
WHOLE SAMPLES OF THE HIGH PRIEST'S READINGS ON EGYPT

Edgar Cayce was a reader of the Bible, which he read it in its entirety over sixty times, from Genesis to the Revelation. He read the King James Version, and somehow his language while giving a reading was in the old King James English, making it difficult for us today to easily read his discourses.

The following are exact copies of some of his dissertations on ancient Egypt and the life of the High Priest Ra-Ta.

TEXT OF READING 294-147 M 55

This psychic reading given by Edgar Cayce at his home on Arctic Crescent, Virginia Beach, Va., this 19th day of July, 1932, in accordance with request made by self—Edgar Cayce.

PRESENT
Edgar Cayce; Gertrude Cayce, Conductor; Gladys Davis, Steno.

READING
Time of Reading 5:30 P.M. ..., Va.

GC: You will have before you the soul-body and the mind of Edgar Cayce, present in this room. You will give a detailed life history of this entity's appearance in Egypt as Ra-Ta, and his associations with those of that period with whom he is closely associated in the present. You will answer the questions which will be asked.

EC: Yes, we have the entity and those conditions or records that are apparent in the inner self of the entity or body in the present, from that as seen and recorded as Ra-Ta the priest.

In giving this interpretation we must find there are many peoples, even nations, that were influenced by the material activities of the entity in that experience.

That the entity came into the land Egypt with others that had come for a purpose is evidenced by that which has been given.

He came with that people from what [Arabia] was to be later the earthly sojourn of the entity as a leader, and as a man then of unusual abilities as well as appearance and manners of conduct.

The entity chose rather the peoples that were to enter in the land, and was the son of a daughter of Zu [See 294-142, Par. 4-A in re Uhjltd and Zu, Ra] that was not begotten of man. In the entrance, then, he came rather as one that was rejected by those peoples about him; for ever has there been that question where such has been the experience among peoples who had formed any associations of home.

Home, as has been remembered, began with a peoples in an entirely different land, and was then projected in thought by those various leaders in those places where man, as man, had come into being through that crystallization of thought that had been given by those Sons of the Most High. [Atlantis?]

In this entity's appearance, then, in this particular experience, there was brought to those peoples of Zu's the condemnation of those of Ararat, [Arart [165]] who had established what would now be called a *community* home in the land later known as Ararat, or where the flood later brought those peoples who again joined with many in peopling the earth after that destruction which was caused by those changes in the land known as Og. [Atlantis? Portion now called Mt. Ararat?]

The entity then grew in grace with the peoples by the manner of conduct, though with the action of those peoples of Ararat these brought hardships for the mother of the entity in that experience, until there had been a change in the environs and brought among a new surrounding. [Egypt]

In this period, then, there was the prophecy by Ra-Ta that the *son* of Ararat [Arart [165]] was to journey into this land where there was then the higher state of developments as to the necessities, and those abilities to enjoy and enjoin the activities of the mental and material bodies in their associated actions. These brought, then, those things that are classed in the present as pleasures that gratify the senses of man's own development, for much that is now as the developments that are necessities as well as luxuries were *then* commonplace as the most common necessities in the present. Hence to those peoples, while Ra-Ta was one that was still looked on askant, with the removal of the peoples into the Egyptian land, during that age of Ra-Ta as would be called today one score and one, then the entity gave much in the way of aiding those peoples, children of Arart and the families of same, in making the easy, even control of a land that might be said to be supplying then all the luxuries of the earth in that particular period.

With the peaceful arrangements that were brought about, then, after the period of dissension with the young natives and the changing of the native's [900's] name to that of the king, Aarat, then the priest [294] was in the position of gradually gathering those that would harken to those words as pertaining to there being any relations with an outside world, or of there being those divisions in the body that were represented by those divisions of the intermission, or the body *of intermission* of an entity, from an experience to an experience. The natives held more strongly to the necessity of materialization for the enjoyment, as may be surmised from the conditions that were surrounded and evidenced in those particular conditions of this period.

With Ra-Ta then beginning with the natives and those that listened to the uncovering of the records (in what would be termed archaeological research in the present), gradually more and more adherence was made to those words of this peculiar leader that had come into this land leading or guiding the conquerors, who were seeking for the expression of various thoughts that were coming through in those entities entering that group in that particular period. This being at that period (as would be called, in the study of such) of the change of the race to become—and is now—the white. Hence, as Ra–Ta means and indicates, among—or the first *pure* white in the experience then of the earth.

In this condition, then, the wonders of the activities brought those varied conditions that were the source of so much disorder, dissension, and discouragement to the activities of the entity through the whole period of experience; for as these findings began to show the variations that had existed in the developing of the mental and physical needs of those peoples that had populated the land, these brought the changes in the manner in which those that had come, as well as natives, in the *way* in which these forces *were to* be expressed in this particular experience.

With the subsiding, then, of contentions with the natives and those that rose against them, and those that had come in the raising to that of what was to be the experimentation (as would be called in the present) of those that were given to Ra–Ta by the king and that native who was to be counseled or judged by those who had been chosen in the positions as the group called (that as would be expressed in the present) the material minded, the spiritual minded, the business minded, the political minded.

These in their divisions, then, made for what may be seen as a *real* representative of the conditions that are arisen in the earth in the present period, when there is the drawing near to that period of a change again, which is as a cycle that has brought about that period when there must be the establishing of that which is in the present the representation of that experimentation for the advancement of those various groups in that particular period.

We are through for the present.

Copy to Self " " File

TEXT OF READING 294-148 M 55
This psychic reading given by Edgar Cayce at his home on Arctic

Crescent, Va. Beach, Va., this 26th day of July, 1932, in accordance with request made by self—Edgar Cayce.

PRESENT

Edgar Cayce; Gertrude Cayce, Conductor; Gladys Davis, Steno.

READING

Time of Reading 5:00 P.M. ..., Va.

(Continuance of Egyptian experience as Ra-Ta)

EC: Yes. With the establishing of this rule, there began the series of changes, and the intermingling of the peoples who entered and the natives. While the native rulers were submissive, especially as the [1734] native ruler was enamored with one of the incoming peoples. With Arart [165] as the king and Ra-Ta as the prophet or seer, there began a period that may well be called a division of interests of the peoples. Ra-Ta attempted to induce the king to have only those natives that were tried and true in their acceptance of those attempts that would bring the closer relationship, according to those visions and experiences of Ra-Ta in line with those being established as customs, rules and regulations. These conditions naturally made for some disturbance among the natives, that would be called the upper class, or those that sought to be in power themselves, or had ideas as to what should be done with the abilities of the peoples as individuals, and the abilities of the country as a country to supply those material necessities for sustenance and for recreation of the peoples.

This eventually led to the pitting of the young leader [900] with the king's son [341], and the change—or the accepting by the king of this native leader that represented a GROUP as well as himself, for he was [900] among those who had been native rulers and were deposed by the ruler [1734] whom Arart had found in office when settling there. This period of the establishing of these conditions we will term, for designation and understanding, as the political situation of the land. A portion of Arart's life then was in association with the political experience, as well as in establishing those relationships of individuals with individuals, also the religious or spiritual life, with preparation for setting in motion the regulations or ceremonies that would be accompanied, or signified or designated, by the developing of those peoples who chose to give their lives, or were chosen for their abilities in certain phases of the conditions that arose.

With the political situation, then, the king [341]—the young king, then only thirty—gathered about him many that were to act in the capacity of council, a portion the inner council that ruled on the general circumstances of the peoples as a whole, then the council that had supervision over various parts of departments of the activities of the peoples, as would be termed in one's present surroundings as holding the various offices as a cabinet, the departments being much in that day as they are in the present; for remember, there is nothing in the present that hasn't existed from the first. Only the *form* or the manner of its use being changed, and many an element then used that the art of its use has been lost, as we will see the reason why, and many being rediscovered by those called scientists in the present when in that day it was the common knowledge of the most illiterate, as would be termed in the present.

With the appointing of such a body, to be sure there was much work for Ra-Ta in council that there be kept the ideal or purpose for which this band, this group, had chosen this particular land for the development or manifestation of the forces that were manifesting through the mental or the spiritual man Ra-Ta.

With this giving in (we are speaking of the political phase now) [of Arart] of the king, to pit or parallel activities of the native with the abilities of the son, or heir, and he himself—the king—acting *as* a council then *with* Ra-Ta to the inner council, there were the necessities of matching the abilities of the king's council, or king's people, with the facilities of the natives—as it were—in the various phases of what would be termed in the present as progress. Hence the opening by Araaraart [341] of mines in Ophir, in what was later known as Kadesh, or in the land now called Persia. Also in the land now known as Abyssinia, and those portions yet undiscovered or used in the upper lands of the river Nile, there were those mines of the precious stones—as onyx, beryl, sardis, diamond, amethyst, opal, and the pearls that came from the sea near what is now called Madagascar. In the northern (or then the southern) land of Egypt, those mines that produced quantities—and quantities—and quantities—of gold, silver, iron, lead, zinc, copper, tin, and the like, that these might be matched with those in the valleys of the upper Nile. Also there was the producing of the stonecutters who began gathering materials for the establishing of the residences of the incoming or the king's peoples.

With the gatherings of these, also Ra-Ta began to gather his own people and those that were pointed out to him through the sources from which he received those various injunctions for the establishing of the name forever in the land. Hence, with these, there were the preparations for the temple where there were to be the various forms of worship, as related to the divisions of the penal or moral relationships of the peoples, and what would be termed or called in the present the religious or spiritual relationships.

There were many periods or days required for the building up of the body, as represented by the group that acted in the capacity of the active individuals about the building of these edifices or temples that were to represent then the recreation halls; for the physical attributes were worshipped much more in many ways in this period than the religious are in the present period, and rightly so—though there were the preparations for the spiritual worship that comprised not only the sacrificial altars, which were not as for the offering of sacrifice in the slaying of animal or bird, or beast, or reptile, or man; rather that upon which individuals put their faults and blotted them out with the fires of those forces that were set in motion by Ra-Ta, in the ability to give to each that for which his or her activity were best adapted in the developing of themselves, when they had chosen to give themselves in service in that particular position in which their activity was necessary. See the difference?

There were also established storehouses, that would be called banks in the present, or places of exchange, that there might be the communications with individuals in varied lands; for even in this period (though much had been lost even by these peoples) was there the exchange of ideas with other lands, as of the Poseidian and Og, as well as the Pyrenean and Sicilian, and those that would now be known as Norway,

China, India, Peru and American. These were not their names in that particular period, but from whence there were being gathered a portion of the recreations of the peoples; for the understandings were of one tongue! There had not been as yet the divisions of tongues in *this* particular land. This was yet only in the Atlantean or Poseidian land.

With the gathering of these people and places, there began the erecting of the edifices that were to house not only the peoples, but the temple of sacrifice, the temple of beauty—that *glorified* the activities of individuals, groups or masses, who had *cleansed* themselves for service. Also the storehouses for the commodities of exchange, as well as that gathered by the peoples to match—as it were, still—one against the other. Hence we find the activities of the priest, or seer, as really a busy life— yet much time was given in keeping self in communion with those that brought the knowledge of that progress made in the spiritual sense in other lands, especially so from Poseida and Og.

In these visitations that were caused, or that necessitated the absenting of the priest from these places, there arose more and more a dissension with those peoples that there was being builded much that was being left to subordinates, as considered by some of the native councillors—and a few also of those that allowed avarice to arise in their own make-up. This brought questioning more and more, and there began to be the use of those things that gradually turned the minds of those associated in the offices that had been set aside by the priest in their activity, in the use of, in the brewing and concocting of drinks that set against the body, set the mind, set the whole fires of physical body against that as had been cleansed by the fires on the altars, as were in the sacrificial temples.

In the third series, or—as they were set aside as periods of ten years, most of those buildings were completed, and when there was the return of Ra-Ta from one of these visits to the mount—where there had been some activities on the part of those that were delving into what was termed the archaeological conditions of those that had lived in the lands in the periods before—and there was found in the temple of sacrifice the aggrandizing of the lusts of the body, rather than those activities that were to be carried on by the sacrificial priests—there arose a mighty turmoil, and with these conditions arising there became greater and greater stress laid upon Ra-Ta, and there were sought various ways and manners in which there might be fault found with the activities of those conditions that surrounded the body, and there arose at that time the first—as may be said—of that saying, "When the devil can't get a man any other way, he sends a woman for him."

Among those, then, of the priests' daughters, was one of the king's favorites—that made for the entertaining of the king and his council, and his visitors—who was more beautiful than the rest, and she [538] was induced to gain the favor of the priest through activities of herself in body, and in the manners that would induce some fault to be found. This was not by her own volition, but rather by the counsel of those that made for the persecutions of her own peoples that were being protected by the activities of the body, and divisions arose that were even unknown then to Ra-Ta, for he being among those that trusted all, believed all, and—as it were—for the time the gods laughed at his weakness!

We are through for the present.

TEXT OF READING 294-149 M 55
This psychic reading given by Edgar Cayce at his home on Arctic Crescent, Va. Beach, Va., this 27th day of July, 1932, in accordance with request made by self—Edgar Cayce.

PRESENT
Edgar Cayce; Gertrude Cayce, Conductor; Gladys Davis, Steno.

READING
Time of Reading 3:15 P.M. ..., Va.

(Continuance of Egyptian experience as Ra-Ta)

EC: Yes, we have that as has been given, and those conditions that surround the body Ra-Ta in that experience.

It will, no doubt, be enlightening to individuals in the present to give the outlines of that which had its being in the varied forms of worship, individuals as beings, their differences in forms from the present, that it may be better understood how these *influences* so much in the present with individual or personal associations of individualities.

The conditions first, then, as political had been set. The conditions as to the buildings (we will call them) in which there was to be carried on this demonstration of the relationships of individuals to individuals, and relationships of individuals as individuals, and as masses, to the Creative Forces.

In the building, then, of the marital relationships that existed, these as we understand, were not much as homes (as seen or understood as individual homes in the present). Rather were there the *appointed* companionships that were to serve their State, their purposes, for the completing of—or competing of—groups or nations one against another, and were rather the matter of the word of the ruler than that of choice of individuals, as known in the present. This particular relationship did the priest, or Ra-Ta, attempt to change, in that there should be rather the establishing of the definite homes, as were in other lands that had been then visited by this priest, or from any; that these should be rather those of consecrated lives one to another. Hence there was the tendency of the changing or altering of those *forms* of service that were held in the temple, in which there were not only those acts in the activities of individuals in their relationships one with another for the propagation of those peoples, but also those recreations, and those—as would be termed in the present—halls of learning, halls of precept and also of examples. These, then, as may be understood, required the supervision—with these changes—of a great number of individuals, and—as is seen from that which has been given—individuals in varied capacities served the priests in ministering to those needs of the conditions and relationships of individuals through the temple; for in this particular peoples all births were in this particular hall—or those set aside for same, as were those chambers in which conception was to have taken place, or to take place, for all the various relationships that existed among the peoples; while in the Temple Beautiful we had rather that which pertained to those changes that were wrought in individuals' activities as they set themselves aside, or consecrated themselves (as would be termed in the present) for particular services in the material or mental, or in the commercial world, as well as those that formed or performed their particular activity or service in the Temple Beautiful, or the spiritual portion of the service.

With these changes, then, that were gradually brought about—possibly a description here of these might be given:

As was seen, the housing of all the female of the whole clan or tribe for the evenings was in the temple, while those of the male that were outside those of the king's own household—and this included the king's alone—not any favorite or queen, or closer relationship, for all were in the same building, for they were under State rules. These were in tiers, as we would term today, beautifully laid out—with their halls, that were three and four tiers. The rooms, as would be sized as we would call, were 7 X 9 in their size, with 8 to 10 feet in the height, with those accoutrements for same—their rugs, their blankets, those that were wrought with the hands that made for the couches, for the various activities. Those that were born in same were immediately, or after three months, taken from their own families and raised in those groups which were confined in other buildings for those purposes. The great chambers or halls that were inter-between were of high tiers, that made for large halls, with the various forms of recreation—as the dance, etc; for, as given, the body was worshipped in this period as sincerely as most of the physical or spiritual worship that may be seen today, for the bodies were changing in their forms as their developments or purifications were effective in those temples, where the consecrations and changes were taking place by the activities of the individuals in their abilities to turn themselves towards (in the mental) the *spiritual* things of an existence. They gradually lost, many feathers from their legs. Many of them lost the hairs from the body, that were gradually taken away. Many gradually began to lose their tails, or their protuberances in their various forms. Many of them gradually lost those forms of the hand and foot, as they were changed from claws—or paws—to those that might be more symmetrical with the body. Hence the activities or the uses of the body, as they became more erect and more active, more shaped to them in their various activities. These were, to be sure, considered as the body beautiful. Beauty as divine; for the divine has brought—and does bring—those various beauties of form or figure to the body, and should be *considered* as it was given so; for "the body is the temple of the living God." True, then, that the various forms or attributes of the body in its symmetry are of the divine inheritance, as was brought about by this ill-forgotten Ra-Ta in this experience.

In the Temple Beautiful, then, we find here the altars where various forms of desire were sacrificed, that brought to the individuals, or persons, or bodies, in the gradual falling away of those things that made for the *animal* activity in the bodies of those that were attempting to so consecrate, so consecrate themselves and consecrate their bodies, their lives, their activities, in this service. Let's don't forget the thesis, or the key for which all of this understanding had come: That there might be a closer relationship of man to the Creator, and of man to man.

Many were the altars, then, and so—as these changes came about—there became the necessity of their attempt to induce Ra-Ta, that there might be more of the activity that was withdrawn, or drawn *to* the bodies of those that were purified, or clarified, in the Temple Beautiful, to draw those to the activities that were to be changing for those that had not reached that stage of the desire to become those changes in the physical and in the mental attributes of that which represented the forms in their activity in the period. Hence the developing more of the *personality*, as these were injected more and more. This is where, as it were, the gods laughed at the weakness of the individual, or the priest.

As these began then, with this favorite of the king—and the better of the forms that had become near the body beautiful, or beauty divine, those activities in the temple (not the Temple Beautiful, but in the temple) brought these individuals, as individuals, into closer relationships, and the decree eventually came that the priest was to be, then, the companion of this body that had been chosen to be the channel through which those activities were to bring to those peoples a body such as the priest had spoken of—and the priest "fell for the whole proposition", to put it in common parlance, or that of slang phrase in the present.

In this there were many others that were chosen also, by the various ones, and there were the attempts that there be the same associations with the priest in the various ones through which this began, yet when there came—as it were—the offspring with this association, then there became the cry that there was the breaking of the very laws that had been set by the priest, who was to make for the home and the changing of the conditions for the peoples, and more and more were the lines drawn as to the sides that were taken. Those groups who had the desire for their own offspring, or their associated or associations for the closer relationships with the priest, and those that came into power in their various forms or activities; for, as is seen, with desire—as the cleansing came—there were those abilities of individuals for various activities in various fields of endeavor. Hence there became singers, workers in linen, workers in embroidery, carders, weavers, workers in clay, those in various forms of commercial industry, those in horticulture, those in agriculture, and the various fields; for no merchants then existed, as there was one common store for all.

In their activities, then, each were in their various fields of endeavor given free activity to that which it might produce. Hence these brought about the many various *divisions* that were between, as it may be called, the first uprising between Church and State, and the lines being drawn caused more tumult, until the period when there was the eventual trial of this priest and the companion, and they were banished into the land that lies to the south and east of this land, or the Nubian land.

Here all became changed, with this tumult that arose with the various priests that were in attendance in the various offices, and advantage was taken of the situation by many of those who in their various forms began to *learn*, as it were, a form of war and defense, and there were the gathering then of the young men, the old men, and sides were taken. Still some remained faithful to the priests who remained in the land, and troublesome times arose for many, many suns, until at least nine seasons had passed before there was even the *semblance* of the beginning of a quieting, and that not until there had been definite arrangements made that the priest *would* return and all would be submissive to his mandates; and he became, then, as may be termed in the present, a dictator—or a monarch in his own right.

The offspring, to be sure, was taken—as others—from this relationship, and in their various forms and manners there was the attempt to be brought about the proper conditions, yet it wasted away—for while there were the abilities of the priest in some directions, yet these had not clarified or crystallized into that which came about in the latter part of this experience for the entity.

In the land to which these were banished, not only were there the two—but a *number*; some two hundred and thirty-one souls.

We are through for the present.

TEXT OF READING 294-150 M 55
This psychic reading given by Edgar Cayce at his home on Arctic Crescent, Va. Beach, Va., this 28th day of July, 1932, in accordance with request made by self—Edgar Cayce.

PRESENT
Edgar Cayce; Gertrude Cayce, Conductor; Gladys Davis, Steno. Mildred Davis.

READING
Time of Reading 4:30 P.M. ..., Va.

(Continuance of Egyptian experience as Ra-Ta)

EC: Yes, we have the information that has been given. With the number that went in exile, of the two hundred thirty and one souls, many were in the capacity of guards, defenders, special body guards, interpreters— not that these interpreters were to interpret languages, or speech, or activities, but give to those that were unable to approach the priest, or body Ra-Ta, that which would be given out where it was impossible for the body to reach all about the body.

With these changes, there became the natural consequences in change of relationships. Pairs were given places of abode, and then homes—with their environs—were first established among those that were sent in exile, or chose of their own volition to be among that number, or who named the name of the priest.

With the entering into the Nubian land, there came such a change that there were the bettered conditions in every term that may be applied to human experience; for successes of every nature grew up about this warlike peoples, and there came those rebellions in the land that made for turmoils and strife. More and more were there overtures made that there be some means provided whereby those who had followed the priest might be *made*, or *forced*, to return; yet these became as insurmountable objections, so that only those who were acting in the capacity of go-betweens of either sex were kept, or able to be in touch with the priest direct. As the priest in this period entered more and more into the closer relationships with the Creative Forces, greater were the abilities for the entity or body Ra-Ta to be able to make or bring about the *material* manifestations of that relationship.

Hence the peace that was enjoyed by the peoples, not only with the priest but all those of that land. Hence, as given respecting individuals, they returned *from* the land, for many sought to be as close in contact with this body as at all possible. Every form of advancement, then, or advantage, seemed to be in the direction that those of the kingdom had acted in haste, and those that were advanced in their purification in the temple—whether they were of the male or female, *with* the ideal of bringing peace to their friends, their peoples, to whom they held some allegiance, kept attempting to make for such associations with the council and the king that there be the re-establishing of the priest in his place in the land.

There were begun some memorials in the Nubian land which still may be seen, even in this period, in the mountains of the land. Whole mountains were honeycombed, and were dug into sufficient to where the perpetual fires are *still* in activity in these various periods, when the priest then began to show the manifestations of those periods of reckoning the longitude (as termed now), latitude, and the activities of the planets and stars, and the various groups of stars, constellations, and the various influences that are held in place, or that *hold* in place those about this particular solar system. Hence in the Nubian land there were first begun the reckoning of those periods when the Sun has its influence upon human life, and let's *remember* that it is in this period when the *present race* has been called into being—and the *influence* is reckoned from all experiences of Ra-Ta, as the effect upon the body physical, the body mental, the body spiritual, or soul body; and these are the reckonings and the effects that were reckoned with, and about, and of, and concerning, in their various phases and effects. These all were set, not by Ra-Ta—but *expressed* in the *development* of Ra-Ta, that these *do* affect—

by the forces as set upon all—not only the inhabitant of a given sphere or planet, but the effect all has upon every form of expression in that sphere of the Creative Energies in action in that given sphere, and this particular sphere—or earth—was the *reckoning* in that period. Hence arose what some termed those idiosyncrasies of planting in the moon, or in the phases of the moon, or of the tides and their effect, or of the calling of an animal in certain phases of the moon or seasons of the year, or of the combining of elements in the mineral kingdom, vegetable kingdom, animal kingdom, in various periods, were *first* discovered or first given, not discovered—first *conscious* of—by Ra-Ta, in his first giving to the peoples of the Nubian land.

Well may it be imagined, then, as to the effect this had upon the peoples who classed themselves as the elect, the chosen, and yet recognizing that for a *physical* activity there had been the envy, selfishness, strife, contention, and those things that are of the body, that pertain to those lusts of the body, which had brought about or produced that which separated that which would build from themselves.

In this condition, then, were there emissaries of the various positions sent back and forth by the leaders of that particular period, that would eventually bring about the restoring of the priest, who—under the strain—very short period had, to the apparent eye of those about him, become aged, decrepit, and not able physically to carry on; and *fear* began to be felt that there would not be the sustaining strength sufficient that there might be given to the peoples that which had been begun by the entity in the Egyptian land, and that which was being manifested in this land to which they had been banished.

Eventually came the period when there was to be the attempt, that there was to be the return of the priest to the land. Then did this priest of himself, and of the Creative Forces, *edict* that those who were in close association with this entity—that had meant an extenuation or savior of a peoples, into a regeneration of same—would have marks set in their bodies that would remain throughout their appearance in the earth's plane, that they might be known to one another, would they seek to know the closer relationships of the self to the Creative Forces and the source—*physical*—of *their* activity *with* that source. To some in the eye, to some in the body, to some the marks upon the body, in those ways and manners that may only be known to those that are in that physical and spiritual attunement with the entity as they pass through the material or earth's sphere together. They are drawn, then, by what? That same element that was being accentuated in the earth's plane, as also the other laws that were discovered—or were given, or were conscious of— by the entity in that particular period. The purpose of such, then, that there may be known, that with such an association there may come an awakening to that which was accomplished by those of the select—not elect, but *select*—in that particular endeavor.

These are, then, in that position wherein their relationships may be of the best, the *closest* relationships of the mental, the material, the *spiritual* developments of all that aided in that particular experience, for the good of the group, the nation, the world—and hence the activities in whatever direction must *influence* the *whole* of the human race, whether *any* of that particular group enter as servants, as kings, as ministers, as those that mete penal justice, or those that would become emissaries, or ministers, or those that are of those sources that in *material* things bespeak of the lore of the attributes of physical relationships. All are to, and for, and *of*, that that makes for an awakening of those conditions, that make for an awareness of that manifested at that period.

With the return then of the priest to the Temple Beautiful, there first began the priest to withdraw himself from the whole that regeneration in body might become manifest, and the body lay down the material weaknesses—and from those sources of regeneration *recreated* the body in its *elemental* forces for the carrying on of that which these material positions gave the opportunity for; leaving first the records of the world from that day until when there is the change in the race.
   Through for the day.

TEXT OF READING 294-151 M 55

This psychic reading given by Edgar Cayce at his home on Arctic Crescent, Virginia Beach, Virginia, this 29th day of July, 1932, in accordance with request made by self—Edgar Cayce.

PRESENT

Edgar Cayce; Gertrude Cayce, Conductor; Gladys Davis, Steno.

READING
Time of Reading 11:00 A.M. ..., Va.

(Continuance of Egyptian experience as Ra–Ta)

EC: Yes, we have the information that has been given respecting the activities of Ra–Ta in the Egyptian experience.

With the completing of this resuscitation, or regeneration of the body–physical, with the return of those that had been forced or had voluntarily followed the priest into exile, with the many that had been healed or changed in the country to which they had been sent, there began then the segregations more into places, homes, and where there had only been forts or temples in the various sections—where the various character of commercial life was carried on gradually grow homes, with families, that were much in the order as may be found in the present day, save there were more than one companion in the various households. These were chosen rather as those that were able to care for, and to bring about those variations in the temperamental forces that were developed during this *developing* period.

In the portion as may be termed the political, with this return—and the necessary changes or alterations in the various sections of this division of the peoples—many changes came about; for, as we find, the native counsellor [Aarat] was rather in the position of the subordinate to the king's demands, or the demands of the *father* of the king, and became rather as a recluse, and shut from much of the activities that were being carried on in the relationships of the nations or peoples with the outside peoples. This made for the rising of others to positions of prominence, or positions of responsibility, in the direction of the exchange of ideas with the outside world; for with the regeneration, more and more became noised abroad that which had been and was being accomplished in this land of plenty, in foods, in ornaments, in the recreation, in the needs of the inner man, in the necessities for the satisfying of desires for the material mind, in the aiding or setting up of the various conditions that are called sciences in the present period.

These made for more and more visitations of the wise men, or the emissaries from the various lands, which heretofore had been visited by this priest Ra-Ta.

In the matter of the temple, or the relationships of man to man, with the change in the home, with the change to the building up of the various sections in or under their own rule, there became the necessity of establishing the rules and regulations that governed the relationships of individuals to individuals, as a criterion, as a measuring stick, as it were, as to what would be the ideal—or that that would be proper and right. These were supervised by those that were close in association with the priest; he, the priest, then acting more and more in the capacity of the advisor, yet not those close in contact save with those that were active as emissaries in the various offices to which these were assigned as the developments began, not only in the place around Luz but also in those cities that were established in the various sections of the land.

As related to the spiritual life, with the establishing then of the home, of the various communities and the various towns and cities, there were also set those in the Temple Beautiful that acted in the capacity of advisors, teachers, ministers, or the ones giving counsel in the spiritual places that were prepared in the various centers. These also made for the gathering together of a group that were set in the various capacities. This of necessity required then, in this department of the work, those of the closer associates with Ra-Ta, as the spiritual messengers that were sent to these various places.

Then began what may be truly termed the first national or nation spirit of a peoples; for with the divisions, rather than this causing a dispersing of ideals or a dividing up of interests, it centralized the interests; for these were being guided by a ruler or king whose authority was not questioned any more, nor were the advisings of the priest questioned, who was acting in rather the capacity of preparing for this very spirit to manifest itself in the way of the national emblems, the national ideas, that stood for the varied activities of not only individuals or groups, but for the general masses. Hence there began the first preparation for what has later become that called The Great Pyramid, that was to be the presentation of that which had been gained by these peoples through the activities of Ra-Ta, who now was known as Ra; for with the entering in of Hermes with Ra—who came as one of the peoples from the mount to which these peoples had been banished—and the raising of that one who had been condemned with the priest in banishment to one that was to be without question the queen, or the advisor to all of her own peoples, there was brought the idea of the preservation of these, not only for those in the present but for the generations that were to come in the experiences and experiences throughout that period, until the changes were to come again in the earth's position that would make for, as it had in this inundation that brought about Ra-Ta's coming in the experience from the gods in the Caspian and the Caucasian mountains, that had brought this change in the peoples. Hence under the authority of Ra, and Hermes as the guide, or the actual (as would be termed in the present) constructing or construction architect with the priest or Ra giving the directions—and those of Isis (now) in the form of the advisor for the laying in of those things that would present to those peoples the *advancement* of the portion of man, or woman, to her position in the activities of the human race or human experience, these changed the position or attitude of these particular peoples as to the position that was held by woman in her relations to the developing of the conditions that either were to be national, local, or individual; for not only does this become then that upon which man depends for those advancements or advents into the material activities, but the nourishing of, the maintaining of, that to which its (the man's) ideals are to be turned in their activity when they arise at that period when expressions are to be given to the active forces in the material activities.

This, then, made for an *endowing* of this body Iso, or Isis, to the position of the first goddess that was so crowned, and there was given then that place that was to be sought by others that would gain counsel and advice even from the priest, gained access through that of Isis to the Throne itself. Not that it rose above the authority of the king, but for that developing necessary for the activities of the woman in those spheres of activity in this particular development.

Then began the laying out of the pyramid and the building of same, the using of those forces that made for the activity of bringing then from those very mountains where there had been those places of refuge that which had been begun to establish these, not only into that which would remain as the place for receiving that which had been offered in the Temple Beautiful on the various altars of the activities of an individual's innate self, but to be the place of initiation of the initiates that were to act in the capacity of leaders in the various activities through this period. This building, as we find, lasted for a period of what is termed now as one hundred years. It was formed according to that which had been worked out by Ra-Ta in the mount as related to the position of the various stars, that acted in the place about which this particular solar system circles in its activity, going towards what? That same name as to which the priest was banished—the constellation of Libra, or to Libya were these people sent. Is it not fitting, then, that these must return? as this priest may develop himself to be in that position, to be in the capacity of a *liberator* of the world in its relationships to individuals in those periods to come; for he must enter again at that period, or in 1998.

In those changes then brought about in these relationships, those who had acted in the capacity of the go-betweens, or the establishing of the closer relationships with Ra-Ta and those acting in the capacity of the leader, or of the council, and of the king himself—then we find the establishing of the king's household; then we find begins the bodily adornment, and the first preparation for such was of the linens that have not as yet been attained in this particular period, since that as was set by those who established this linen development from the cottons, and the hemp, and the papyrus flowers and lotus flowers of this particular period.

In and with these became the preparing of the Temple Beautiful for a more perfect place of preservation of those things that were to make known later in the minds of peoples, as the changes came about in the earth, the rise and fall of the nations were to be depicted in this same temple that was to act as an interpreter for that which had been, that which is, and that which is to be, in the material plane.

We are through for the present.

TEXT OF READING 294-152 M 55

This psychic reading given by Edgar Cayce at his home on Arctic Crescent, Virginia Beach, Virginia, this 29th day of July, 1932, in accordance with request made by self—Edgar Cayce.

PRESENT

Edgar Cayce; Gertrude Cayce, Conductor; Gladys Davis, Steno.

READING

Time of Reading 4:45 P.M. ..., Va.

(Continuance of Egyptian experience as Ra–Ta)

EC: Yes, we have the information that has been given. With the building of that memorial, there were the developments in many—or every—other line of human experience and development. These were the natural development of the ideal that was held by the entity Ra–Ta from the beginning, for these were man's relationship to his Maker, man's relationship to his fellow man.

As this memorial progressed, so did the progression in the activities of individuals and groups grow. As has been intimated in the types of homes, of cities, of every character of physical, mental and spiritual manifestations. The symbolized ideas in the homes, in the buildings, and the acceptance of this, that or the other that contributed to the welfare of man, found an individual that claimed—or set about to, in some form, add that to *their* contribution of man's development. Hence as the Ibex, the scarab, the sacred ox, the sun, the eagle, and those in nature of every character that aided or abetted in representing an ideal of an individual brought into prominence by their ability to preserve same in some manner or form.

The decorations in Temple Beautiful became more elaborate. These, with the supervision of Isis (now), and with the spiritual influence of Iso, [See 378-16, Par. 6, on 10/29/33] brought more and more attendance of that part of man's development. As did also in the temple of recreation, where NOW only those that had gained that position where their bodies in form presented the human form divine, or the lines that were seen by the carvers in stone, the workers in brass, the moulders in iron, the wrought in gold of Ra, and those women that aided and assisted in the ministering to the individuals through the guiding of those truths found by their continued association with the spiritual truths that more and more became apparent in their physical activities.

Also there were then with those of Ra born other children, that were to rise in their various capacities, that their activities would be carried on. With this again brought contentions among the civil and political factions of the land. This again brought the disturbing forces in Ra, and there came then that period when all the pyramid or memorial was complete, that he, Ra, ascended into the mount and was borne away.

Ready for questions.

(Q) As each of the following individuals are named, you will give my association and relationship with each at that time, and the attitude I should bear to each in the present for our best development. First, Araaraart—[341]: (A) As given, the king; and the attitude as ever—those of a fearful understanding, that makes for the continued advancement or the continued activity toward that which brings contention. How may these be for the best development? United in the one cause, for the development of the fellow man in its relationships to the Creative Forces in the universe, and their activity in same, and the relationships of man to man.

(Q) Isris—[538]: [See 538-30 on 9/3/31.] (A) As in the experience, that which brought for the attempt to bring into material existence that as the representation of *ideals* in the spiritual mind, so may there be brought in the present associations the perfecting of relationships to ideals, both in the material, the mental and spiritual sense.

Each have their burden to bear. Each have their lesson to learn. Each have their goal to attain.

(Q) Iso—[288]: (A) As the entity was then that which represented not only an *ideal* in the material form, but offered a channel that brought the relationships that assisted, in being an entity *and* an ideal in the manifested material form, hence in the present the associations that bring about the perfecting of relationships of the Creative Forces with man, and man's relationships to one another, these relationships must be in that manner, that form, that brings same into an *ideal* activity.

(Q) Islta—[295]: (A) As these entities, and this entity in particular, represented the bringing of those relationships with those peoples that were at variance to that attempted, so will there be in the present those relationships that, nourished in the manner as indicated in those forces as promised in those set in body and mind, there may be the perfecting of that return where all phases of man's experience may be brought to the knowledge and understanding of those that seek to know His face. For even as was in that experience, the body, the mind, the entity, brought those associations that meant much for the opportunities of relationships one with another, in groups, in masses, so may the association in the present bring about those activities in *that* direction.

(Q) It–Cit—[243]: (A) The relationships then were afar, yet physically in the defense oft one of another; for, as may be seen in those relationships then:

Each as a material or physical individual depended upon the entity Ra–Ta for mental, material and spiritual sustenance. Each in the present has sought, has found, material and physical assistance. Make the *mental and spiritual one!*

We are through for the present.

TEXT OF READING 294-153 M 55

This psychic reading given by Edgar Cayce at his home on Arctic Crescent, Va. Beach, Va., this 4th day of August, 1932, in accordance with request made by self—Edgar Cayce.

PRESENT

Edgar Cayce; Gertrude Cayce, Conductor; Gladys Davis, Steno. Mildred Davis.

READING

Time of Reading 4:10 P.M. ..., Va.

(Soul and body mind of EC—continuing with associations and relationships with each during his appearance in Egypt as Ra–Ta, as named, giving attitude he should bear to each in present for best development)

(Q) [340]—as Arhira: (A) Yes, we have those conditions mental and material that surrounded the body–physical known as Ra–Ta, or Ra, in Egypt.

In the associations or contacts with individuals in the present, many and far reaching are the influences. There are many that make for those close impending forces in the activities of those that were drawn by those bonds that were creative in their nature in that association. There are many that make for urges hard to be understood in the material surroundings of the present, by those who know not of that that must have passed through those of that experience, which made for binding of souls in their associations for developments or hardships, or the variations as they are known in the material-plane at this particular period. Those who have received that sign in themselves, in the manner that may be known to them in their activities, may be bound together for the building of soul forces that make for the closer union with Creative Forces, and find expressions in the material affections in the manner that brings a manifestation of that being activated in theirselves.

The one given, then, may be as an illustration of this. *Then* the entity was *bodily* in close association, yet on account of conditions materially was far from the closeness that would make for an appreciation of the opportunity held in that experience. Hence in this, as in others, as has been seen, there is a dependence in a manner that is not able to be gotten away from, either in physical or mental. Hence the attitudes should be as those of a building in each that makes for an understanding of those neglects that must be taken account of.

(Q) [348]—as Pti-Rai: (A) One associated in the position rather as of awe. Not of consternation, but as inability of physically showing the appreciation of the position. Hence again will there be a seeking for that which may bring an awakening in the mental forces of the association—succor for the soul, for the body!

(Q) [2112]—Al-Lai: (A) In this we find an example of how the body fought against that which became an impelling influence in the experience, and chose to attempt to of itself claim forces that made for disruption in the experience. In the present may there be found awe and belief, yet that same impelling influence that it may be the stronger alone. The power that came was not of Ra, not of Ra-Ta. Neither may the powers that may be made manifest be of *any* individual's making; for the individual is only chosen vessel for the manifestation of *His* power—and the vessel may *not* be broken by not claiming for self powers within self. Through the *humbleness* of self may the manifestations of His power be the greater.

(Q) [69]—Isaholli: (A) In the associations in the service, in the active forces of both the material associations and the spiritual cleansings; and will work together for the good of many in activative forces that have been hindered through other experiences. These are well.

(Q) [[69]'s husband]—Minister & prophet: (A) Not in that experience.

(Q) [307]—Islao: (A) As one giving out those things builded, and a close follower of and an aid to many in service. "He that would be the greatest will be the servant of all."

(Q) [404]—As-Razh: (A) As one of the natives caused a lot of disorder, eventually coming to a closer association when the return brought better relations in the activities of all. *Much* may be gained one from the other by the applications in the present of the *tenets* of that experience. God is One! God is Spirit, and seeks such to worship Him.

(Q) [993]—Iskxe: (A) Close in associations in the Temple Beautiful. Those activities of the entity aided *many* in gaining an understanding of the truths, as related to the spiritual manifestations shown by *material* activities. Hence their associations are *strong*. Strong attachments grew up then. Strong associations by their activities may be expected in the present. Much good may be accomplished in union of their strength.

(Q) [560]—Isusi: (A) One who faltered, yet gained much with those activities in those experiences and associations in that period. Joining more in the activities in the *temple* than in the sacrificial activities. More, then, may be expected in the *material* activities that make for a closer *understanding* towards the spiritual.

(Q) [115]—Itasldhoia: (A) The one that made for much loud speaking in many places.

Became one of the chief emissaries. One that caused much disorder among those that were not of the faith, those that were brought in; *aiding* much throughout the replenishing, the rebuilding, the regenerating, and came in close association with those especially that *builded* materially, and later spiritually, in the local and in other lands. Much aid may come, and much disorder may be expected—by those activities that are *not understood* by others, as was in that experience.

(Q) [303]—Islex: (A) One who gained, yet again fell away—with the disorders that arose. Gradually coming back, through those experiences in the regenerating and rebuilding in the portion of both entities' experiences. Much aid may be had to each by their concerted efforts in aiding others. That's a lot! Put it together!

(Q) [413]—Li-Los: (A) An aide in the temple, and not *closely* associated—but much aid came to those the entity Ra-Ta would help, through the material activities of the entity.

(Q) [2673]—Ra-Tu: (A) A very close association, *especially* with the return; for the entity was of those who came *with* the activities, *seeing* much of that in the banishment; bringing much to many, building *strong*—and one of the most powerful of her sex, among certain peoples, in that experience. Hence a special activity may be expected, at unexpected places and times.

(Q) [2124]—Pa-Rizla: (A) Among those who resisted, or follow with many of those in the activities that aided—and yet led many to believe, or to follow in taking their positions or stands; later becoming an assistant that aided in an upbuilding of *commercial* forces, and for *self*—advancement *and* losses. In the present much may be gained by a close cooperation.

(Q) [2125]—Arisis: (A) Of those peoples who aided in the distribution of those activities, and much may come by the associations in study of those experiences.

(Q) [311]—Ich-Li-En: (A) This a later period than the closer activities of those that came in personal contact. These brought much that aided many, for this entity became then a student OF those things being put in the pyramids. He should be an interpreter OF that given, to many.

(Q) [462]—Arlea: (A) An aide in many manners that brought others' activities, rather than self—though the associations are well through the *mental*. The *mental* associations will make for an expanding in the *influences* of each.

(Q) [301]—Isibio: (A) In the close association, as of the offspring that made for the *demonstrating* of the activities of the mental, the material and spiritual aspects. Bringing *joy* to many, and in the associations may bring an awakening to many in the present.

(Q) [275]—Ai-Si: (A) One of the musicians that made for the activities in the Temple Beautiful, as well as in the temple that aided much. Each will seek from the other.

(Q) [165]—Arart: (A) Counseled oft. Called to be the one to give much.

One who failed much. One who gained much. Their lives, or their lines, will meet oft—and diverge oft. Much may be gained in the *mental* associations.

(Q) [953]—Asriaio: (A) Of the resisting forces oft to Ra-Ta, and also those that gathered with those who builded. Hence there were builded then many conditions that respond in the present as peculiar activities, as related to individuals and particular groups. Much may be gained. Much will be *given* by each in their varied associations.

(Q) [900]—Aarart: (A) One that gathered *with* the activities in the first portion of the building up of conditions there, being of the natives. Then brought much resistance and degrading to self through the activities, when there were the misunderstandings during the banishments—and these were for the discharging of the activities in those direct experiences that made for barriers that are hard to be overcome. Their activities diverged, then came together—faulty in both's return.

(Q) [257]—Arsha: (A) A close associate in many of the activities, both before and after the rebellions had been put down. Saved from the offering of unholy fire on the altars in the temple, and the rejection of same. Losing self in that, and retained only by Ra—in the replenishing and rebuilding, when his name was changed then to Su-Su-Bo. When the change, then, has come, the associations will be closer in their mental and spiritual activities—for they will be drawn along lines under persecution. We are through for the present.

The next Cayce discourses contain material about the Great Pyramid.

TEXT OF READING 5748-5

This psychic reading given by Edgar Cayce at his home on Arctic Crescent, Virginia Beach, Va., this 30th day of June, 1932, in accordance with request made those present of the Norfolk Study Group #1 and friends, of the Ass'n for Research & Enlightenment, Inc., during the Annual Congress of the Association.

PRESENT

Edgar Cayce; Gertrude Cayce, Conductor; Gladys Davis, Steno. Norfolk Study Group #1 and friends.

READING
Time of Reading 3:00 P.M.

GC: You will please give at this time detailed information regarding the origin, purpose and prophecies of the Great Pyramid of Gizeh near Cairo, Egypt. Please answer the questions asked.

EC: Yes. In the information as respecting the pyramids, their purpose in the experience of the peoples, in the period when there was the rebuilding of the priest during the return in the land, some 10,500 before the coming of the Christ into the land, there was first that attempt to restore and to add to that which had been begun on what is called the Sphinx, and the treasure or storehouse facing same, between this and the Nile, in which those records were kept by Arart and Araaraart in the period.

Then, with Hermes and Ra (those that assumed or took up the work of Araaraart) there began the building of that now called Gizeh, with which those prophecies that had been in the Temple of Records and the Temple Beautiful were builded, in the building of this that was to be the hall of the initiates of that sometimes referred to as the White Brotherhood.

This, then, receives all the records from the beginnings of that given by the priest, Arart, Araaraart and Ra, to that period when there is to be the change in the earth's position and the return of the Great Initiate to that and other lands for the folding up of those prophecies that are depicted there. (All changes that came in the religious thought in the world are shown there, in the variations in which the passage through same is reached, from the base to the top—or to the open tomb *and* the top. These are signified by both the layer and the color in what direction the turn is made.)

This, then, is the purpose for the record and the meaning to be interpreted by those that have come and do come as the teachers of the various periods, in the experience of this present position, of the activity of the spheres, of the earth.

In the period that is to come, this ends—as to that point which is between what is termed in chronological time in present—between 1950 and '58, but there have been portions that have been removed by those that desecrated many of those other records in the same land. This was rejected by that Pharaoh who hindered in the peoples leaving the land.

(Q) Are the deductions and conclusions arrived at by D. Davidson and H. Aldersmith in their book on The Great Pyramid correct?

(A) Many of these that have been taken as deductions are correct. Many are far overdrawn. Only an initiate may understand.

(Q) What corrections for the period of the 20th century?

(A) Only those that there will be an upheaval in '36.

(Q) Do you mean there will be an upheaval in '36 as recorded in the pyramid?

(A) As recorded in the pyramid, though this is set for a correction, which, as has been given, is between '32 AND '38—the correction would be, for this—as seen—is '36—for it is in many—these run from specific days; for, as has been seen, there are periods when even the hour, day, year, place, country, nation, town, and individuals are pointed out. That's how correct are many of those prophecies as made.

Oft may there be changes that bring periods, as seen in that period when there was an alteration in that initiate in the land of Zu and Ra that brought a change, but at a different point because of being driven by those that were set as the guides or guards of same.

In this same pyramid did the Great Initiate, the Master, take those last of the Brotherhood degrees with John, the forerunner of Him, at that place. As is indicated in that period where entrance is shown to be in that land that was set apart, as that promised to that peculiar peoples, as were rejected—as is shown in that portion when there is the turning back from the raising up of Xerxes as the deliverer from an unknown tongue or land, and again is there seen that this occurs in the entrance of the Messiah in this period—1998.

TEXT OF READING 5748-6

This Psychic Reading given by Edgar Cayce at his home on Arctic Crescent, Virginia Beach, Va., this 1st day of July, 1932, in accordance with request made by those present of the Norfolk Study Group #1 and friends, of the Association for Research and Enlightenment, Inc., during the Annual Congress of the Associations.

PRESENT

Edgar Cayce; Gertrude Cayce, Conductor; Gladys Davis, Steno. Norfolk Study Group #1 and friends.

READING

Time of Reading 4:10 P.M. Eastern Standard Time.

EC: [See 5748-6, Par. B1.] Much has been written respecting that represented in the Great Pyramid, and the record that may be read by those who would seek to know more concerning the relationships that have existed, that may exist, that do exist, between those of the Creative Forces that are manifest in the material world. As indicated, there were periods when a much closer relationship existed, or rather should it be said, there was a much better understanding of the relationship that *exists* between the creature and the Creator.

In those conditions that are signified in the way through the pyramid, as of periods through which the world has passed and is passing, as related to the religious or the spiritual experiences of man—the period of the present is represented by the low passage or depression showing a downward tendency, as indicated by the variations in the character of stone used. This might be termed in the present as the Cruciatarian Age [?]*, or that in which preparations are being made for the beginning of a new sub-race, or a change, which—as indicated from the astronomical or numerical conditions—dates from the latter portion or middle portion of the present fall [1932]. In October there will be a period in which the benevolent influences of Jupiter and Uranus will be stronger, which—from an astrological viewpoint—will bring a greater interest in occult or mystic influences.

At the correct time accurate imaginary lines can be drawn from the opening of the great Pyramid to the second star in the Great Dipper,

---

*[From Webster's Standard Dictionary of obsolete words: cruciat: a crusade; also, a papal bull sanctioning a crusade or privileging participants in it; cruciatory torturing; tormenting.]

called Polaris or the North Star. This indicates it is the system toward which the soul takes it flight after having completed its sojourn through this solar system. In October there will be seen the first variation in the position of the polar star in relation to the lines from the Great Pyramid. The dipper is gradually changing, and when this change becomes noticeable—as might be calculated from the Pyramid—there will be the beginning of the change in the races. There will come a greater influx of souls from the Atlantean, Lemurian, La, Ur or Da civilizations. These conditions are indicated in this turn in the journey through the pyramid.

How was this begun? Who was given that this should be a record of man's experiences in this root race? for that is the period covered by the prophecies in the pyramid. This was given to Ra and Hermes in that period during the reign of Araaraart when there were many who sought to bring to man a better understanding of the close relationship between the Creative Forces and that created, between man and man, and man and his Maker.

Only those who have been called may truly understand. Who then has been called? Whosoever will make himself a channel may be raised to that of a blessing that is all that entity-body is able to comprehend. Who, having his whole measure full, would desire more does so to his own undoing.

(Q) What are the correct interpretations of the indications in the Great Pyramid regarding the time when the present depression will end?

(A) The changes as indicated and outlined are for the latter part of the present year [1932]. As far as depression is concerned, this is not—as in the minds of many—because fear has arisen, but rather that, when fear has arisen in the hearts of the created, *sin* lieth at the door. Then, the change will occur—or that seeking will make the definite change—in the latter portion of the present year. Not that times financially will be better, but the minds of the people will be fitted to the conditions better.

(Q) What was the date of the actual beginning and ending of the construction of the Great Pyramid?

(A) Was one hundred years in construction. Begun and completed in the period of Araaraart's time, with Hermes and Ra.

(Q) What was the date B.C. of that period?

(A) 10,490 to 10,390 before the Prince entered into Egypt.

(Q) What definite details are indicated as to what will happen after we enter the period of the King's Chamber?

(A) When the bridegroom is at hand, all do rejoice. When we enter that understanding of being in the King's presence, with that of the mental seeking, the joy, the buoyancy, the new understanding, the new life, through the period.

(Q) What is the significance of the empty sarcophagus?

(A) That there will be no more death. Don't misunderstand or misinterpret! but the *interpreation* of death will be made plain.

(Q) If the Armageddon is foretold in the Great Pyramid, please give a description of it and the date of its beginning and ending.

(A) Not in what is left there. It will be as a thousand years, with the fighting in the air, and—as has been—between those returning to and those leaving the earth.

(Q) What will be the type and extent of the upheaval in '36?

(A) The wars, the upheavals in the interior of the earth, and the shifting of same by the differentiation in the axis as respecting the positions from the Polaris center [See *Earth Changes* booklet report, p. 30, published by E.C.F. in 1963].

(Q) Is there not a verse of scripture in Isaiah mentioning the rock on which the great pyramid is builded?

(A) Not as we find; rather the rock on which John *viewed* the New Jerusalem—that is, as of the entering in the King's Chamber in the Pyramid.

(Q) What is the date, as recorded by the Pyramid, of entering in the King's Chamber?

(A) '38 to '58.

(Q) If the Passion of Jesus is recorded in the Great Pyramid, please give the date according to our present system of recording time?

(A) This has already been presented in a fair and equitable manner through those students of same, and these descriptions have been presented as to their authenticity.

(Q) How was this particular Great Pyramid of Gizeh built?

(A) By the use of those forces in nature as make for iron to swim. Stone floats in the air in the same manner. This will be discovered in '58

[See *Earch Changes* booklet report pages 33–34, E.C.F. 1963].

(Q) What is the significance of the character of the figure of the Sphinx, mentioned above?

(A) In this particular period of Araaraart and of the priest (that began those understandings—and passed through those of the hell in the misinterpretation of same), there was even then the seeking through those channels that are today called archaeological research.

In those periods when the first change had come in the position of the land, there had been an egress of peoples—or *things* as would be called today—from the Atlantean land, when the Nile (or Nole, then) emptied into what is now the Atlantic Ocean, on the Congo end of the country. What is now as the Sahara was a fertile land, a city that was builded in the edge of the land, a city of those that worshipped the sun—for the use of its rays were used for supplying from the elements that which is required in the present to be grown through a season; or the abilities to use both those of introgression and retrogression—and mostly retrograded, as we are in the present. The beginnings of these mounds were as an interpretation of that which was crustating in the land. (See, most of the people had tails then!) In those beginnings these were left.

When there was the entrance of Arart and Araaraart, they begin to build upon those mounds which were discovered through research. With the storehouse, or record house (where the records are still to be uncovered), there is a chamber or passage from the right forepaw to this entrance of the record chamber, or record tomb. (This may not be entered without an understanding, for those that were left as guards may *not* be passed until after a period of their regeneration in the Mount, or the fifth root race begins.)

In the building of the pyramid, and that which is now called the Mystery of Mysteries, this was intended to be a *memorial*—as would be termed today—to that counsellor who ruled or governed, or who acted in the capacity of the director in the *material* things in the land. With the return of the priest (as it had been stopped), this was later—by Isis, the queen, or the daughter of Ra—turned so as to present to those peoples in that land the relationships of man and the animal or carnal world with those changes that fade or fall away in their various effect. These may be seen in a different manner presented in many of the various sphinxes, as called, in other portions of the land—as the lion with the man, the various forms of wing, or characterizations in their various developments. These were as presentations of those projections that had been handed down in their various developments of that which becomes man—as in the present.

We are through.

* * *

Transcripts of Edgar Cayce's readings are housed at his ongoing center, located at 215 67th Street in Virginia Beach, VA, 23451. His Web site is www.EdgarCayce.org.

Appendix C

MORE FACTS ABOUT THE GREAT PYRAMID

The number of stone blocks in the Great Pyramid has been estimated at 2,300,000 weighing from two to thirty tons each with some weighing as much as seventy tons. The Great Pyramid sits on thirteen acres with each side of the pyramid covering a little over five acres in area. Amazingly, each of these sides slopes in to a centerline with an extraordinary degree of precision, causing the pyramid to actually have eight sides. It is the only pyramid to have concave sides. (See illustration 3.)

In its original condition there were roughly 144,000 casing stones covering the pyramid, all highly polished and flat to an accuracy of 1/100th of an inch and with nearly perfect right angles for all six sides. The average casing stone on the lowest level was 5 ft. long by 5 ft. high by 6 ft. deep and weighed fifteen tons. The larger casing stones weighing as much as twenty tons were placed with an accuracy of 5/1000ths of an inch, and an intentional gap of about 2/100ths of an inch allowed for the use a special mortar.

The mortar used in the Great Pyramid is of an unknown origin. It has been analyzed and its chemical composition is known, but it cannot be reproduced. Stronger than the stone, it still remains intact today. The cornerstone foundations of the pyramid have ball and socket construction capable of dealing with heat expansion and earthquakes.

The length of a base is 9,131 PI (Pyramid Inch) from corner to corner in a straight line. The length of a base side at the base socket level is 9,131 pyramid inches or 365.24 pyramid cubits. The length of a base side at sidereal socket level is 9,131.4 pyramid inches or 365.256+ pyramid cubits.

The top surface is 5,478 pyramid inches above the mean socket level. Another 335 pyramid inches higher is the geometric apex formed by the corner edges of the projected original siding (which is missing). The 35th course of stones is roughly 50 inches tall, nearly twice the height of the previous courses. The height of the 35th course = 1,162.6 PI from ground or the length of the Antechamber x 10.

The Great Pyramid is the only pyramid to have chambers above ground level, and only the Great Pyramid has shafts coming off of its major chambers. The King's Chamber has two, about 5 inches in diameter that connect to the exterior of the pyramid, indicating that they are airshafts. Why would a chamber with a coffin in it need air? The likely answer is that the chamber was used by incarnate, breathing initiates in a death–like ceremony that revealed the nature of life beyond physical life, leaving the initiates wiser. We see the same effect on people today who have had a near–death experience, NDE. They return with a peace towards their lives and circumstances with no fear of dying.

The Queen's Chamber has two shafts that do not reach completely to the exterior. The cross section of these shafts is sometimes oval, sometimes domed, and sometimes rectangular. 213.25 feet (65 meters) up the southern shaft of the Queen's Chamber is a miniature portcullis slab discovered by a robotic camera in 1993. Attached are two copper fittings, one broken. This area of the shaft is lined with Tura limestone, which is typically used in pyramids only for lining chambers.

In the King's Chamber all of the stone joints are very tight except in the lower left-hand corner of the west wall. Here the joints are larger than normal and covered by mortar. This is a strong indication of an opening to another chamber or passage. The Egyptian government has refused requests for further exploration.

In 1986 a French team using microgravimeter equipment detected small hidden cavities behind the west wall of the horizontal passage to the Queen's Chamber. They were permitted to bore two 1" diameter holes and found a cavity filled with sand. They were not permitted to dig or tunnel for further investigation. The sand was not indigenous to Giza. Where did it come from and why is it there? These questions remain unanswered. These cavities correspond to two floor stones in this passageway with joints perpendicular to the rest of the joints in the floor stones. This type of indicator can also be found at the junction of the descending and ascending passageways, indicating again that there may be more unopened passageways and chambers in the Great Pyramid.

In 1987 a Japanese team used an electromagnetic wave method to search for cavities in the Great Pyramid. They identified a cavity under the horizontal passage to the Queen's Chamber about 1.5 meters beneath and extending for 2.5–3.0 meters in depth. They also identified a cavity behind the western part of the northern wall of the Queen's Chamber. They identified no cavities within the King's Chamber, possibly due to the denser granite walls. Three potential cavities were identified in the area of the Sphinx. This alignment is corresponds to the Duat; a common practice in ancient Egypt, where the structures of the earth are positioned to mirror the architecture of heavens.

About seventy feet along the north side of the Great Pyramid from the northeast corner is a 4' x10' stone sunk into the foundation at an angle. The joints are very precise, and this is the only stone in the foundation perimeter not at a right angle to normal construction. It would have been hidden by the original limestone casing stones, but it is now accessible. It is very likely an entrance. Yet, no further investigation has been done.

It has long been believed that the Sphinx had subterranean tunnels leading to each of the three major pyramids. In October, 1994, a passage leading to a subterranean area beneath the Sphinx was re-discovered.

The information encoded into the Great Pyramid is repeated multiple times. With the polished white limestone casing stones in place, the Great Pyramid could be seen from the mountains in Israel and probably the moon as well. Its polished surfaces would have reflected light of the moon and Sun like a beacon.

It is so well constructed and so massive that the average temperature inside the Queen's Chamber was a steady 68 degrees Fahrenheit (that was before thousands of tourists and their body heat entered the pyramid each day).

The Great Pyramid was used to indicate solstices and equinoxes. The pyramid is located at 29 degrees, 58 minutes, 51.06 seconds north latitude, and 31 degrees, 9 minutes, and 0.0 seconds east longitude. It marks the Spring Equinox in a most curious way: Due to the angle of the sides of the pyramid vs. its latitude, it casts no shadow at noon during the spring equinox. It is aligned True North; the most accurately aligned structure in existence and faces true north with only 3/60th of a degree of error. The position of the North Pole moves over time and the pyramid was probably exactly aligned at one time.

More Specifications:

- The height of the pyramid to the missing apex formed by extending the sides is 5,813 PI. The height of the pyramid without the capstone is 5,496 PI.
- The five angles of the Great Pyramid are: edge to edge of face at apex = 76:17:13.2 (degrees: minutes: seconds), edge to diagonal edge at apex = 96:3:0.0, dihedral or face to face parallel to base = 112:25:39.4, edge to base = 41:59:50.5 face to base = 51:51:14.3. The face to base angle is the angle of the casing stones.
- The volume of the pyramid is: V = 1/3 base area x height = 161,559,817,000 cubic PI = 10,339,828.3 cubic pyramid cubits {(5813.2355653 PI)/3 * 9131 PI * 9131 PI}
- The Great Pyramid's corner edges are 8688.00 PI in length.
- The slant face height of the Great Pyramid's sides is 7391.72 PI.
- The area of the base covers 13.3 acres or 83,375,161 sq. PI.
- The area of each face covers 10.8 acres or 67,493,782 sq. PI.
- The angle of the Descending Passage is 26 deg, 18 min, 9.5 sec or about 26.30 degrees.

- The passages are straight to within 0.013 in. per 100 ft.
- The dimensions of the Descending Passage are 4535 PI in length, 41.524 PI in width, and 36.197 PI in height. [4:197]
- The length of the Ascending Passage from the junction of the Descending Passage to the Grand Gallery is 1543.46451 PI.
- The length of a base side is 9131 pyramid inches measured at the mean socket level, or 365.24 pyramid cubits, which is the number of days in a year, accurate to 5 digits.
- The perimeter of the base divided by 100 = 365.24, the number of days in a year, accurate to 5 digits.
- The length of the Antechamber used as the diameter of a circle produces a circumference of 365.242, accurate to 6 digits.
- The length of the granite portion of the floor of the antechamber to the King's Chamber times $2*\text{sqrt(Pi)} = 365.242$
- The ratio of the lengths of the Grand Gallery to the solid diagonal of the King's Chamber times 100 equals the number of days in a tropical year, accurate to 8 digits.
- The height of the pyramid times $10^{**}9$ = avg. distance to sun. [$5813.2355653 * 10^{**}9 * (1 \text{ mi} / 63291.58 \text{ PI}) = 91,848,500$ mi] Mean Distance to the Sun: Half of the length of the diagonal of the base times $10^{**}6$ = average distance to the sun Mean Distance to Sun: The height of the pyramid times $10^{**}9$ represents the mean radius of the earth's orbit around the sun, or Astronomical Unit. [5813.235565376 pyramid inches x $10^{**}9 = 91,848,816.9$ miles] Mean Distance to Moon: The length of the Jubilee passage times 7 times $10^{**}7$ is the mean distance to the moon. [$215.973053 \text{ PI} * 7 * 10^{**}7 = 1.5118e10 \text{ PI} = 238,865$ miles]
- Sun's Radius: Twice the perimeter of the bottom of the granite coffer times $10^{**}8$ is the sun's mean radius. [$270.45378502 \text{ PI}* 10^{**}8 = 427,316$ miles]
- Earth's Polar Radius: The sacred cubit times $10^{**}7$ = polar radius of the earth is the distance from North Pole to Earth's center [25 PI $* 10^{**}7 * (1.001081 \text{ in.} / 1 \text{ PI}) * (1 \text{ ft.} / 12 \text{ in.}) * (1 \text{ mi.}/ 5280 \text{ ft.}) = 3950$ miles].
- Radius of the Earth: The curvature designed into the faces of the pyramid exactly matches the radius of the earth.

- The sum of the pyramid's two base diagonals in PI = length of the Precession of the Equinoxes (~25827 years) Precession of the Equinoxes:
- The distance from the ceiling of the King's Chamber to the apex of the pyramid = 4110.5 PI. Which is the radius of a circle whose circumference = the precession of the equinoxes. {4110.5 * 2 * Pi= 25827}
- The perimeter of the 35th course of blocks, which is much thicker than any of the other courses, gives a figure for the precession of the equinoxes. Average Land Height:
- The average height of land above sea level for the earth is 5449 inches. This is also the height of the pyramid.
- On midnight of the autumnal equinox in the year of the Great Pyramid's completion, a line extending from the apex pointed to the star Alcyone.
- Our solar system is thought by some to revolve around this star along with other solar systems much like the planets revolve around our sun.
- A line drawn on a map from the apex of the pyramid to Bethlehem = angle of the Ascending Passage and crosses the Red Sea at the most likely point that the Israelites crossed when departing Egypt (Parting of the Red Sea).
- A line drawn on a map south from the apex of the pyramid at the angle of the Ascending Passage crosses Mount Sinai (Ten Commandments).
- North Star Pointer:

   The Descending Passage pointed to the pole star Alpha Draconis, ca 2170–2144 BC. This was the North Star at that point in time. No other star has aligned with the passage since then.

   The 344 ft. length of the Descending Passage provides an angle of view of only +/– 1/3 of a degree. Alpha Draconis has not been in alignment for thousands of years. The next alignment with the North Star, Polaris, was in 2004 AD.
- The southern shaft in the King's Chamber (45 deg, 00 min, 00 sec) pointed to the star Al Nitak (Zeta Orionis) in the constellation Orion, ca 2450 BC.

- The Orion constellation was associated with the Egyptian god Osiris.
- No other star aligned with this shaft during that Epoch.
- The northern shaft in the King's Chamber (32 deg, 28 min, 00 sec) pointed to the star Alpha Draconis, ca 2450 BC.
- The southern shaft in the Queen's Chamber (39 deg, 30 min, 00 sec) pointed to the star Sirius, circa 2450 BC. Sirius was associated with the Egyptian goddess Isis and is also part of a unique ceremony practiced by the African Dogon tribe.
- The northern shaft in the Queen's Chamber (39 deg, 00 min, 00 sec) pointed to the star Ursa Minor, ca 2450 BC.
- Five of the seven brightest stars have pyramid equivalents: The three great pyramids of Khufu, Khafra, and Menkaura for the belt of Orion; the pyramid of Nebka at Abu Rawash corresponds to the star Saiph; the pyramid at Zawat al Aryan corresponds to the star Bellatrix. The only two missing star positions are for Betelgeuse and Rigel.

Bibliography

1. Adams, W. Marsham. *The House of the Hidden Places: A Clue to the Creed of Early Egypt from Egyptian Sources.* Originally published in 1895. Whitefish, MT: Kessinger Publishing, LLC, 2010.

2. Bauval, Robert, and Adrian Gilbert. *The Orion Mystery.* New York, NY: Random House, 1995.

3. Bonwick, Tomes (1817–1906). *Egyptian Belief and Modern Thought.* London: C.K. Paul, 1978.

4. Breasted, J.H. *Ancient Records of Egypt, Vol I.* Chicago: University of Chicago Press, 1906.

5. Budge, E.A. Wallis. *The Book of the Dead: The Papryus of Ani.* Originally published in 1895. New York, NY: Dover Publications, 1967.

6. ———. *The Egyptian Heaven and Hell.* 3 volumes. Originally published in 1905. New York, NY: Dover Publications, 1996.

7. ———. *Egyptian Magic.* Originally published in 1894. Whitefish, MT: Kessinger Publishing, LLC, 2010.

8. ———. *Osiris and the Egyptian Resurrection.* Originally published in 1911. New York, NY: Dover Publications, 1973.

9. Capt, E. Raymond. *A Study in Pyramidology.* Thousand Oaks, CA: Artisan Sales, 1986.

10. Collins, Andrew. *The Cygnus Mystery.* New York, NY: Sterling Publishing, 2007.

11. Cruttenden, Walter. *Lost Star of Myth and Time.* Pittsburg, PA: St. Lynn's Press, 2006.

12. Davidson, David and Aldersmith, H. *The Great Pyramid: Its Divine Message.* London: Williams and Norgate, Ltd., First Edition 1924, Eleventh Edition 1948.

13. Edgar, John and Morton Edgar. *Great Pyramid Passages: Part II, Letters from Egypt and Palestine.* London: Bone & Hulley, 1913.

14. ———. *Great Pyramid Passages: Vol. I.* Glasgow: Bone & Hulley, 1923. [note: originally published in 1910 in London, but revised in 1923]

15. Evelyn-White, Hugh G., trans. *Hesiod, Homeric Hymns, Epic Cycle, Homerica.* New York: G. P. Putnam's Sons, 1922; Bartleby.com, 2010. www.bartleby.com/241/103.html.

16. Faulkner, R.O. *The Ancient Egyptian Coffin Texts*, Vols. 1–3. Modern Egyptology Series. Warminster, England: Aris & Phillips, 2004.

17. Faulkner, R.O., Ogden Goelet, Carol Andrews, and James Wasserman. *The Egyptian Book of the Dead: The Book of Going Forth by Day—The Complete Papyrus of Ani Featuring Integrated Text and Full-Color Images.* San Francisco: Chronicle Books, 1994.

18. Fergusson, James. *A History of Architecture in All Countries, from the Earliest Times to the Present Day, Vol. 1 (Classic Reprint).* Reprinted by Hong Kong: Forgotten Books, 2012.

19. Gardiner, A.H.: *The Admonitions of an Egyptian Sage from a Hieratic Papyrus in Leiden.* J.C. Hinrich's che Buchhandlung, 1909; reprinted by George Olms Verlag, 1969; reprinted by General Books LLC, January 12, 2010.

20. Greaves, John. *The First Book of the Pyramids: Pyramidographia.* Great Britain, 1646.

21. ———. *Miscellaneous Works of Mr. John Greaves.* Oxford, 1737. Reprinted in Memphis, Tennessee: General Books, 2010.

22. Herodotus. *The Histories. Vol. II.* Translated by Sir Henry C. Rawlinson. London: John Murray Publishing Co., 1852.

23. Herz-Fischler, Roger. *The Shape of the Great Pyramid.* Waterloo, Ontario, Canada: Wilfrid Laurier University Press, 2000, initially published in 1940.

24. Lachman, Gary. *The Quest for Hermes Trismegistus.* Edinburgh, Great Britain: Floris Books, 2011.

25. Lemesurier, Peter. *The Great Pyramid Decoded.* Shaftesbury Dorset, United Kingdom: Element Books, 1977. Revised and Expanded Edition, Barnes & Noble 1996.

26. Lepre, J.P. *The Egyptian Pyramids: A Comprehensive, Illustrated Reference.* Jefferson, NC: McFarland & Company, 2006.

27. Maspero, Gaston. "La Religion Égyptienne." *Revue de l'Histoire des Religions* (1884), t. xii, 125.

28. Newtown, Isaac Sir. Article "A Dissertation upon the Sacred Cubit of the Jews and the Cubits of the several Nations." Web addresshttp://www.newtonproject.sussex.ac.uk/view/texts/diplomatic/THEM00276.

29. NOVA. *Magnetic Storm.* PBS airdate: November 18, 2003. Transcript: http://www.pbs.org/wgbh/nova/transcripts/3016_magnetic.html.

30. Petrie, Sir William Matthew Flinders. *The Pyramids and Temples of Gizeh.* Chestnut Hill, MA: Elibron Classics, Adamant Media Corporation, 2007.

31. Rutherford, Adam. *Pyramidology Book I: Elements of Pyramidology.* Hertfordshire, United Kingdom: The Institute of Pyramidology, First Edition 1957, Second Edition 1961.

32. ———. *Pyramidology Book II: The Glory of Christ as Revealed by the Great Pyramid.* Hertfordshire, United Kingdom: The Institute of Pyramidology, 1962.

33. Smyth, Charles Piazzi. *Our Inheritance in the Great Pyramid.* London: Wm. Isbister, Limited, 1880.

34. ———. *The Great Pyramid: Its Secrets and Mysteries Revealed.* "Fourth and Much Enlarged Edition." Originally titled: *Our Inheritance in the Great Pyramid.* New York: Bell Publishing Company, 1978.

35. Stevenson, Ian. *Twenty Cases Suggestive of Reincarnation.* Charlottesville, VA: University Press of Virginia, First Edition 1966, Second Edition 1974.

36. ———. *Reincarnation and Biology: A Contribution to the Etiology of Birthmarks and Birth Defects Volume 1: Birthmarks.* Westport, Connecticut, and London: Praeger Publishers, 1997.

37. ———. *Reincarnation and Biology: A Contribution to the Etiology of Birthmarks and Birth Defects Volume 2: Birth Defects and Other Anomalies.* Westport, Connecticut, and London: Praeger Publishers, 1997.

38. Strabo. *The Geography of Strabo.* Vol. III. Translated by H.L. Jones. Originally published by London: W. Heinemann and reprinted by New York, G. P. Putnam's Sons, 1917.

39. Van Auken, John. *Edgar Cayce's Tales of Ancient Egypt.* Virginia Beach, VA: A.R.E. Press, 2011.

40. Vyse, Howard. *Operations Carried on at the Pyramids of Gizeh in 1837. Vol. II.* London: James Fraser, 1840, 1842.
41. Wake, Charles Staniland. *The Origins and Significance of the Great Pyramid.* London: Reeves & Turner, 1882.

Index

R

reincarnation 55, 81, 82, 83
Rosetta Stone 8, 15, 32

S

Sayce, Archibald Henry 34
Shaw, John 94
Sington, David 94
Smyth, Charles Piazzi 18, 23, 24,
     61
Solinus, Julius 6, 7
Sprenger, Alois (Aloys) 16
Stadelmann, Rainer 10
stars 3, 15, 16, 22, 41, 48, 62, 63,
     64, 65, 76, 78, 92, 123, 139,
     145, 167

Stevenson, Ian 81, 82
Strabo 6, 64

T

Taylor, John 23
Tibetan Book of the Dead 17, 51

V

Vyse, Howard 11, 16

W

WGBH in Boston 93

4TH DIMENSION PRESS

An Imprint of A.R.E. Press

4th Dimension Press is an imprint of A.R.E. Press, the publishing division of Edgar Cayce's Association for Research and Enlightenment (A.R.E.).

We publish books, DVDs, and CDs in the fields of intuition, psychic abilities, ancient mysteries, philosophy, comparative religious studies, personal and spiritual development, and holistic health.

For more information, or to receive a catalog, contact us by mail, phone, or online at:

4th Dimension Press
215 67th Street
Virginia Beach, VA 23451-2061
800-333-4499

4THDIMENSIONPRESS.COM

Who Was Edgar Cayce?
Twentieth Century Psychic and Medical Clairvoyant

Edgar Cayce (pronounced Kay-Cee, 1877-1945) has been called the "sleeping prophet," the "father of holistic medicine," and the most-documented psychic of the 20th century. For more than 40 years of his adult life, Cayce gave psychic "readings" to thousands of seekers while in an unconscious state, diagnosing illnesses and revealing lives lived in the past and prophecies yet to come. But who, exactly, was Edgar Cayce?

Cayce was born on a farm in Hopkinsville, Kentucky, in 1877, and his psychic abilities began to appear as early as his childhood. He was able to see and talk to his late grandfather's spirit, and often played with "imaginary friends" whom he said were spirits on the other side. He also displayed an uncanny ability to memorize the pages of a book simply by sleeping on it. These gifts labeled the young Cayce as strange, but all Cayce really wanted was to help others, especially children.

Later in life, Cayce would find that he had the ability to put himself into a sleep-like state by lying down on a couch, closing his eyes, and folding his hands over his stomach. In this state of relaxation and meditation, he was able to place his mind in contact with all time and space—the universal consciousness, also known as the super-conscious mind. From there, he could respond to questions as broad as, "What are the secrets of the universe?" and "What is my purpose in life?" to as specific as, "What can I do to help my arthritis?" and "How were the pyramids of Egypt built?" His responses to these questions came to be called "readings," and their insights offer practical help and advice to individuals even today.

The majority of Edgar Cayce's readings deal with holistic health and the treatment of illness. Yet, although best known for this material, the sleeping Cayce did not seem to be limited to concerns about the physical body. In fact, in their entirety, the readings discuss an astonishing 10,000 different topics. This vast array of subject matter can be narrowed down into a smaller group of topics that, when compiled together, deal with the following five categories: (1) Health-Related Information; (2) Philosophy and Reincarnation; (3) Dreams and Dream Interpretation; (4) ESP and Psychic Phenomena; and (5) Spiritual Growth, Meditation, and Prayer.

Learn more at EdgarCayce.org.

What Is A.R.E.?

Edgar Cayce founded the non-profit Association for Research and Enlightenment (A.R.E.) in 1931, to explore spirituality, holistic health, intuition, dream interpretation, psychic development, reincarnation, and ancient mysteries—all subjects that frequently came up in the more than 14,000 documented psychic readings given by Cayce.

The Mission of the A.R.E. is to help people transform their lives for the better, through research, education, and application of core concepts found in the Edgar Cayce readings and kindred materials that seek to manifest the love of God and all people and promote the purposefulness of life, the oneness of God, the spiritual nature of humankind, and the connection of body, mind, and spirit.

With an international headquarters in Virginia Beach, Va., a regional headquarters in Houston, regional representatives throughout the U.S., Edgar Cayce Centers in more than thirty countries, and individual members in more than seventy countries, the A.R.E. community is a global network of individuals.

A.R.E. conferences, international tours, camps for children and adults, regional activities, and study groups allow like-minded people to gather for educational and fellowship opportunities worldwide.

A.R.E. offers membership benefits and services that include a quarterly body-mind-spirit member magazine, *Venture Inward*, a member newsletter covering the major topics of the readings, and access to the entire set of readings in an exclusive online database.

Learn more at EdgarCayce.org.

EDGARCAYCE.ORG